MAHABHARATA

FOR CHILDREN

MAHABHARATA

FOR CHILDREN

ARSHIA SATTAR

ILLUSTRATED BY SONALI ZOHRA

juggernaut

JUGGERNAUT BOOKS
C-I-128, First Floor, Sangam Vihar, Near Holi Chowk,
New Delhi 110 080, India

First published in hardback by Juggernaut Books 2020
Published in paperback by Juggernaut Books 2024

10 9 8 7 6 5 4 3 2 1

P-ISBN: 9789353457143
E-ISBN: 9789353451288

Typeset by R. Ajith Kumar

For sale in the Indian Subcontinent only

Printed at Thomson Press India Ltd

Contents

The Beginning

Deep in the forest that is filled with singing birds and darting deer and curious hare, you can hear the distant trumpeting of elephants and the roars of lions and tigers. But the soft water-music of streams will lead you to pools filled with lotuses that are surrounded by trees hanging low, laden with sweet fruit. The fragrance of flowers fills the air, gentle breezes rise and fall in the early mornings and late evenings, following the sun as he marks day from night in his journey across the sky. The forest is peaceful, the forest is a place where we can be close to the world that the gods made, the forest is a place where even time stops to breathe.

A group of sages lived in a forest like this. They ate what the forest gave them, they bathed in the cool waters of the lotus pools, they focused their minds on what was true and good and beautiful. And in the evenings, they gathered to talk about the past, the present and the future. On one such evening, a young sage named Ugrashravas, who had just returned from the city, had a great story to tell.

It is the story that we now call the Mahabharata. It is a story of a great war, of a family torn apart by greed and ambition and jealousy, a story of kings and princes and brave heroes, a story about queens and fearless women who fought for what they wanted, a story about a man who held god within himself, a story about how good people do bad things and how bad people are honourable, it is a story about who we are and who we can be. It is a story that we still tell today.

In that quiet gathering of sages who already knew the best of things and the worst of things, Ugrashravas took a deep breath and then he spoke in a voice that was clear as a bell.

Ugrashravas said:

In the rich and prosperous city of Hastinapura, King Janamejaya was conducting a sacrifice like no other. It was a grand ceremony that would give him what he wished for. Hundreds upon hundreds of priests recited the sacred words that brought the gods to earth, thousands upon thousands of people came to enjoy all that the city had to offer – the marketplaces that overflowed with silks and jewelled ornaments and spices from faraway lands and wooden toys painted in bright colours and glass bangles that caught the light of the lamps at night, the acrobats and clowns and jugglers and actors and singers and dancers, the cattle and horse fairs and the bazaar of strange animals.

It was a time of celebration but the sacred ritual itself was dark and bitter. Janamejaya wanted to avenge the killing of his father by the snake Takshaka, and so he was performing the sarpa satra, a ceremony that brought the snakes from the three worlds into the burning fire pit at the heart of the sacrificial altar. Helpless against the powerful spells and mantras uttered by the priests, snakes who lived on land and in water, in the deserts and in the places where nothing grew, those who

lived underground and in deep mountain caves, those who had their homes in trees and in the grasslands came – none of them could fight the magic words that were pulling them to their horrible, painful death.

Along with their wives and children, their families and their old parents, the snakes slithered and tumbled into the flames of Janamejaya's sacrifice, hissing in agony.

It was there, at this sacrifice, that I heard this story from the wise Vaishampayana who heard it from Vyasa, the greatest of all storytellers, who saw it all unfold before his very eyes. It is said that when Vyasa wanted his great story to be written down, it was elephant-headed Ganesha himself who descended from the heavens to write it as Vyasa recited it.

Let me tell you what I heard from Vaishampayana.

Vaishampayana said:

Once, long ago, there was a good and just king named Shantanu. He was born in the line of the great Bharata kings and ruled from Hastinapura, the city of his forefathers. One day, when Shantanu was wandering in the pleasant lands outside his city, he saw a woman standing by the banks of the river Ganga. He was curious about who she was, alone and far from where people live. As he drew closer, he became certain that she was the most beautiful woman he had ever seen. His heart pounded loudly in his ears and his mouth grew dry because he realised that even though he knew nothing about her, he was going to ask her to marry him.

He bowed to her and said, 'Lovely lady, you have captured my heart. I know that I cannot live without you. Marry me. I am the king of Hastinapura, I am rich and powerful but it is my love for you that will give you the best of everything on earth.'

'I can marry you only on one condition, good king,' said the woman. 'You must never ever question anything that I do. Can you agree to that?'

Noble Shantanu stood tall and squared his shoulders. 'My lady, it shall be as you say. I will never question you. This is the promise I give you as I ask you to be mine.'

The woman placed her hand in his without any hesitation. It was as soft and as delicate as a flower. Shantanu took his new beloved back to his palace and they were married with all the rituals and ceremonies that ensured their happiness, their long lives and the birth of many sons.

Shantanu and the woman he had found by the river were, indeed, happy together and soon she gave birth to a beautiful boy. Shantanu was overjoyed. He showered his wife with gifts and looked forward to teaching his son how to become a great warrior and a good king. But when the child turned a year old, his mother took him to the river and drowned him. Grief burned in Shantanu's heart and made it difficult for him to breathe, but he recalled the promise he had made and said nothing to his wife. Year after year, a sweet, smiling boy would be born to Shantanu and his queen and, each time, the queen would take their son away and drown him.

This happened seven times and finally Shantanu couldn't bear it any longer.

When their eighth child was born, Shantanu cried out, 'What kind of woman are you? Which mother drowns her own children? How can you do this? Give me my son!'

'You have broken your promise, my husband,' she said quietly and her eyes filled with tears as she turned to the man she had loved for so many years.

'I don't care about my promise to you! How can I not question you when you are doing something so heartless?' replied Shantanu, trembling.

'I will tell you why I have drowned our sons,' she said. 'I am the goddess Ganga. These boys born to us are the Vasus, celestial beings who accompany the gods Indra and Vishnu. They were cursed to be born on earth because they were mischievous and stole sage Vasishtha's cow. I was appointed by the gods to give birth to them and let them live only for a year. By killing them, I have been setting them free so that they can return to their homes.'

Shantanu placed his head at her feet. 'How could I have known, sweet wife, great goddess!' he whispered. 'Forgive me. I will never question you again.'

Ganga smiled sadly as she raised the king from the ground. 'I, too, must leave you now. My time on earth is done, I have fulfilled the task I was set.'

Shantanu wept and begged her not to go. Ganga consoled him and said, 'Our last son, the eighth Vasu, must live on earth for his entire life. His curse was different from that of the others. I will take him with me to heaven now. But when he has learned all that he must, I will send him back to you. He will be the living symbol of the love we have shared and he will be with you for as long as you live.'

Ganga gently wiped the tears from Shantanu's face and then she picked up her infant son and vanished.

Shantanu continued to rule his kingdom wisely and well but there was no joy in his life. He often walked by the river, remembering the woman he had loved. Years passed in this way and then, one day, Shantanu noticed that the river looked different. Instead of the clear deep waters that he was accustomed to, the river appeared shallow and muddy. He followed the river's course and came to a bend where he saw a boy shooting arrows into the water that blocked the river's normal, smooth flow.

The youth shone with an inner light, his eyes were clear and his arms were strong and steady. Shantanu hailed him. He asked him who he was and what he was doing. But before his astonished eyes, the boy disappeared. In a flash, Shantanu understood that this was his eighth son, the one that Ganga had taken away with her. Raising his voice to the heavens, Shantanu called out to his wife.

Ganga appeared, as lovely as ever, her presence as soothing as her cool waters on a hot day. The boy was with her. She said, 'This is our youngest son, Shantanu. Take him back to Hastinapura. He will grow up to be a wise man and a great warrior – the divine sages have been his teachers.'

Shantanu embraced his son and together they returned to the city, where Shantanu anointed him heir to the throne. He called him Gangadatta, 'the gift of Ganga', so that he would always remember his wife. The people rejoiced when they saw their beloved king smiling again and they welcomed their new prince with open hearts.

Years went by and Gangadatta grew into a fine young man. He was calm, he was learned and, with his great strength and many skills, he was unrivalled in battle. His reputation spread far and wide and he was admired by all. Gangadatta had a quiet love for his father, he noticed his moods and took care of his needs. And so Gangadatta was concerned when he saw that Shantanu was looking pale and thin, that he had lost interest in the affairs of the kingdom. He seemed not to eat or sleep and he sighed heavily all the time.

Gently, Gangadatta said to him, 'Father, is there something wrong? The kingdom is prosperous, our people are happy, no enemies threaten our borders. But you are troubled. Tell me what is on your mind.'

Shantanu kissed his son on the forehead and said, 'You are a good man, my son. But there is nothing you can do to ease my cares.'

Gangadatta said, 'Tell me, father, tell me so that I can find a way to help you.'

Shantanu sighed. Staring at the ground, he spoke. 'The other day, I was walking by the river, as usual, and I was overcome by a heavenly fragrance. I had never smelled anything like it, it took over my senses, it made my hands shake, my legs quiver. I followed that divine smell and found a young woman, a fisherman's daughter, sitting by her boat. The smell came from her, the air around her was so heavy with it, I nearly fainted. I fell in love with her, son, I knew I could not live without that fragrance in my life. I asked her father for her hand in marriage and he agreed. But the woman said that she would marry me only if her sons would inherit the throne and rule Hastinapura after me.'

'What is the problem with that?' asked Gangadatta.

Shantanu raised his eyes to look at his son. 'You will rule the land of the Bharatas after me, Gangadatta, you are my firstborn son. I have anointed you my heir in public. You are the worthiest successor any father could ask for. This is your kingdom. I cannot take it away from you.'

When Gangadatta smiled, he looked like his mother. He said, 'Father, this kingdom means nothing to me. I give up all claims to the throne from this moment onwards. Take me to your lady of the heavenly fragrance. I will tell her myself that her sons will be kings and that I shall never challenge them for the throne.'

Shantanu said, 'But what about your sons, my son? Whatever you do, your children will always have a right to the throne. And what about the sons of your sons? Your solution could place our family in danger for generations to come. I cannot accept your offer. It will make me happy now, but what of the future?'

Gangadatta placed his hand on his heart and said, 'Father, I swear upon my divine mother and upon my love for you, I shall never marry, I shall never have children. There will never be any rivals to the sons of the fisherman's daughter for the throne of the Bharatas!'

The earth shook when he finished speaking, flowers fell from the sky and a chorus of voices rang out. 'Hail, Gangadatta! The world will now know you as Bhishma, the Awesome, because of the difficult promise that you have made. The gods respect you and the entire world will hold you in great esteem. Bhishma, the gods grant you a boon: you can choose the moment of your death! Live in glory, Bhishma! You will be remembered forever.'

The very next day, Bhishma went with his father to claim the fisherman's daughter as the king's new bride. When the woman came to the palace of Hastinapura, she was known to everyone as Queen Satyavati.

Rivals for the Throne

Ugrashravas said:

Before she became Satyavati, the fisherman's daughter had been an ordinary girl who helped her father in his work. She often ferried people from one side of the river to the other in the boat her father owned. Like her people, she smelled of the work she did, she smelled of fish and she was named for that smell – Matsyagandha. One day, a sage came to the riverbank and asked to be taken to the other shore. The fisherman was busy and so he told his daughter to stop mending their nets and take the sage across the river.

Matsyagandha did as she was told, but when they got to the middle of the river, the sage stopped the boat and, with his powers, created a mist that covered the boat completely. The mist was cool and dark and it made it impossible to see what lay ahead. Matsyagandha was puzzled and looked at the sage, wondering what he had in mind. The sage said to her, 'I am pleased with you, young woman. I give you the boon of a son who will be a powerful sage, like me. He will tell the greatest story the world has ever heard and he will be remembered long after his death as Vyasa!'

At once, a young man appeared – he was dressed in rough clothes of bark, his hair was long and wild, his beard was flecked with glints of copper, but his eyes were deep and dark and seemed to hold within them the wisdom of the ages. He bowed to his mother and said, 'I will live in the forest, mother. But I will never be far from you. When you need me, think of me and I will come to your side.'

Matsyagandha could barely believe what was happening and she said to the sage, 'Thank you for this full-grown son who has gone off to live in the forest. I am sure he will come to me when I ask. But now, may

I ask you for a boon, something that I would like?' The sage smiled. Quickly, the fisherman's daughter spoke. 'My name is Matsyagandha and I smell of fish. I want to smell beautiful, I want to smell more lovely, more sweet than all the flowers on earth and in heaven!'

In an instant, a fragrance unlike anything ever before filled the air. It was so enchanting that even the mist covering the boat stirred, as if to inhale it. Matsyagandha thanked the sage, the mist lifted and they crossed the river to the other shore. The fisherman's daughter was never called Matsyagandha again.

Vaishampayana said:

Satyavati and Shantanu had two sons and Bhishma treated them as if they were his own. After Shantanu died, Bhishma taught them what he knew – how to be just and righteous, how to pay attention to the welfare of the citizens, how to wield their bows and arrows, their swords and their spears. The elder son, Chitrangada, grew to be a great warrior, but while he was still a young man, he was killed in a skirmish with the celestial gandharvas. The second prince, Vichitravirya, became king at a young age and soon Satyavati asked Bhishma for his advice about a suitable bride for her son.

Bhishma thought for a while and then he said, 'The king of Kashi has three beautiful daughters. I will bring them back as brides for our young prince.'

Since the entire world knew of Bhishma's skills as a warrior, no one challenged him when he kidnapped the three princesses, Amba, Ambika and Ambalika, and brought them to Hastinapura. Ambika and Ambalika were excited and seemed happy to become part of the Kaurava court, so famous in all the three worlds. But Amba came to Bhishma, weeping. She said, 'Bhishma, let me go, I have given my heart to another man and he, too, has promised himself to me. Don't consign me to an unhappy life in this kingdom. My sisters will be good wives to your brother!' Bhishma was moved by the young woman's plea and set her free to return to the man she loved.

The new brides brought joy and renewed energy into the family but misfortune continued to stalk the Kauravas. Vichitravirya was struck down by a mysterious illness and died, leaving his wives childless.

Again, Satyavati went to Bhishma, but this time she did not ask for his advice or his help. She said, 'I have another son, a brother to the sons of this kingdom who both died so young. He is a great sage, like his father. I will ask him to ensure that the throne of Hastinapura has an heir.' Bhishma did not argue with his father's wife.

Satyavati closed her eyes and thought of the son she had seen only once in her life. In her mind, she called his name and, at once, he stood before her.

Vyasa looked older than when she had last seen him, but he seemed as wild as before, almost like a forest animal. With a start, Satyavati realised that her firstborn son was not at all pleasant to behold; in fact, his appearance was really quite disturbing. She calmed herself and smiled at Vyasa, who said, 'I am here, mother. What can I do to help you?'

Satyavati made him sit on a comfortable seat and ordered fruit for him to eat, milk for him to drink and water to wash his feet. 'Son,' she said, 'with your great powers, you know everything. You know that the Kauravas are in danger as our kings, your brothers, have died without producing heirs. Vichitravirya's wives are childless, the kingdom has no future.'

Vyasa said, 'You have nothing to worry about, mother. I will visit Ambika tonight and Ambalika tomorrow night. Tell them to receive me with courtesy, for I am your firstborn son and the elder brother of their husband.'

That same night, Vyasa went to Ambika's chambers where she was waiting for him. But when she saw the sage with his wild hair, his uncut nails, his leathery skin and his unusual clothes which carried the smell of the dark forest, she closed her eyes in fright. Vyasa said, 'I have promised my mother that I will give you a mighty, powerful son, but because you closed your eyes when you saw me, Ambika, your son will be born blind!'

Ambika burst into tears but Vyasa had already left the room. Ambika managed to warn her sister about the sage's appearance and so, the next night, when Vyasa went to visit Ambalika, the younger princess was prepared. But even then, the blood drained from her face when she saw Vyasa. 'You are pale, Ambalika,' said Vyasa. 'Perhaps my face is not to your liking. Never mind. You, too, shall have a son. He will be king. But he will be white, as pale as the waning moon, as pale as watery milk, as pale as the empty clouds that carry no rain within them.'

Vyasa told his mother that he had performed his duty to her and to his brothers and now it was time for him to return to the forest and continue with his life of penance and meditation. Satyavati was disappointed that her grandsons would be less than perfect, but she hid her feelings and blessed Vyasa as he left the palace.

Months later, the palace rejoiced when two beautiful boys were born, as Vyasa had promised. But the elder one was blind and the younger one was pale, paler than the silk cloth in which he was wrapped. The blind child was named Dhritarashtra and the younger child was named Pandu. The boys grew up together, each taking care of the other. Again, it was Bhishma who became a parent to these fatherless boys and brought them up with love and affection. He was gentle when he played with them but stern and demanding when he watched them learn how to use weapons and study the sacred texts. Satyavati was never far from her grandsons and she watched them

with a sense of deep satisfaction, knowing that they were under wise Bhishma's protection.

Dhritarashtra and Pandu grew up and both of them were trained by the best of teachers that Bhishma had found for them. He ruled the kingdom in their name until they were old enough to be crowned. Because Dhritarashtra was blind, Pandu became king of the Kaurava lands. Though he was the ruler, Pandu consulted Dhritarashtra on all matters of state and gave him the respect that he deserved as an elder brother.

Bhishma chose the king of Gandhara's daughter as a bride for Dhritarashtra because she had a great boon – she would be the mother of one hundred sons. When Bhishma went to bring her to her new home, he saw that a young boy, lame in one leg, clung to her and wept as if his heart was breaking. 'Who is this?' he asked gruffly.

Gandhari stammered that he was the brother that she had cared for since he was born. 'He knows no family other than me,' she said quietly.

'Bring him with you. He's nothing but a weak, mewling puppy!' Bhishma said and turned away to call for the chariot that would take the young bride to Hastinapura, where she would spend the rest of her life.

It was only when she was being anointed with sweet-smelling oils and adorned with jewels in preparation for the wedding ceremony that Gandhari learned the man she was going to marry was blind. He had never seen the sun set or the moon rise, the sky at dawn, the light playing on the waters of a stream, flowers that blazed with colour in the summer or the lightning that flashed across dark clouds during a storm. This man, her husband, would never ever see her beautiful face.

Gandhari made a terrible decision. She asked her maid to bring her a piece of silk. She said, 'Cover my eyes. Bind this cloth around my face tightly so that not even a sliver of light can penetrate it. I, too, shall be blind, like my husband. I will share the darkness into which he was born.'

Far away from Hastinapura, in the western regions ruled by a powerful Yadava clan, there was a young girl named Kunti. When she was old enough, her family organised a swayamvara for her, a ceremony in which a royal woman could choose her own husband from all the princes that gathered to win her hand. Kunti chose Pandu and she, too, came to live in the Kaurava kingdom. Pandu married again, the princess of Madra, who was known as Madri. She was a beautiful young woman, with lotus-shaped eyes and skin the colour of molten gold. Pandu loved her very much but she would be the cause of his death.

Like so many other kings, one day, Pandu went hunting in the forest and killed a pair of deer. But the deer were actually a powerful sage and his wife who had taken on this animal form so that they could enjoy the pleasures of the forest with each other. With his last breath, the sage cursed Pandu. 'You have killed us, a loving couple who meant you no harm! If you ever approach your wives with love in your heart, you too, shall die!'

The curse weighed heavily on Pandu. He handed the throne of

Hastinapura to Dhritarashtra and Bhishma and went to live a simple life in the forest with his two wives.

After Pandu and his wives had left for the forest, Gandhari got pregnant and the entire palace waited with bated breath for the child to be born, for her pregnancy was extraordinarily long, much longer than the usual nine months. Pandu could not be happy when he heard this news, because he longed for children of his own. What he did not know was that Kunti, too, had a boon that would ensure the birth of sons. When Kunti saw how depressed her husband was, she decided it was time to share her secret with him. She said, 'Dear husband, I have a way of lifting this sadness from your face. Listen. I can call upon any of the gods to give me a son.' Pandu was overjoyed and said, 'Let us not waste any time!'

Kunti and Pandu decided that their first son should be given to them by Dharma, the god of righteousness, so that he would rule wisely and well when he became king. They named their eldest son Yudhishthira. For their second son, they called upon Vayu, god of the wind, who was strong and courageous and a great fighter. They wanted their son to be like him. When the child was born, he was very large and so they named him Bhima. Kunti called upon handsome Indra, lithe and agile, the god of the storm winds, to give her a third son. She named him Arjuna.

Madri grew anxious when she saw Kunti and Pandu rejoice in their children. She begged Kunti to share her boon so that she, Madri, would not be left without sons. Kunti was not pleased but she said, 'You can use this boon only once!' and shared the magic words with her. Madri called the Ashwins and gave birth to the twins Nakula and Sahadeva.

After Yudhishthira was born to Kunti and Pandu, Gandhari could bear her endless pregnancy no longer, for she had wanted to give birth to the eldest prince in the family. In her anger and frustration, she beat her swollen belly with her fists, hoping to force the child out of her womb. But all that came out of her body was a solid ball of flesh. Gandhari wept and wailed and tore her hair. Quickly, Satyavati called to her son Vyasa in her mind. He arrived, panting and sweating, but in a second, he knew what had happened.

He consoled the young queen and said, 'All is not lost, Gandhari. Your boon of a hundred sons will be fulfilled. Cut this ball of flesh into one hundred pieces. Place them in one hundred clay pots filled with oil and let them lie quiet for some months. Your sons will be born safely and will grow up to be strong and healthy.'

When Gandhari's first son was born, jackals howled and enormous owls flapped their wings and hooted. Wild animals gathered at the city gates and meteors blazed through the skies. A fierce wind arose and all the lamps in the palace flickered and went out. The people of the palace shuddered and trembled at these terrifying omens and they whispered among themselves, 'Gandhari's firstborn will destroy us all. He should not be allowed to live!'

Gandhari heard them, but she held her child tightly against her bosom and kissed his forehead. She named him Duryodhana. Ninety-nine other sons came from the clay pots but Gandhari loved Duryodhana most of all.

One Hundred and Five Princes

Ugrashravas said:

Kunti's boon to have sons from the gods was a powerful one. She had received it before she was married, when she was a young girl living in her uncle's house. One day, a sage came to stay and Kunti's uncle told her to look after him with great care. Kunti devoted herself to the sage and looked after his every comfort and wish. He was pleased with her and gave her the boon as a reward for all that she had done for him. Kunti was thrilled and decided to check if it really worked.

One morning, she saw the rising sun and was awed by its glorious splendour. She called upon Surya, the sun god, to give her a child. Soon, she held a shining infant in her arms. He was as radiant as his father and was born wearing gleaming earrings. His body was covered in bright armour and he dazzled the eyes with the light that he carried within himself. Kunti panicked when she realised what she had done – how would she, an unmarried girl, explain this child to anyone?

With tears streaming from her eyes, she held her son close for the last time. She walked to the river and placed him in a basket that she found on the shore and let him float away to whatever fate held in store for him. Later, she married Pandu and had her three other sons – Yudhishthira, Bhima and Arjuna. But the sight of the rising sun always made her sad and she never forgot the child who had shone so brightly in her young arms for a brief moment.

Vaishampayana said:

Kunti, Madri, Pandu and their five sons lived simply in the forest while Dhritarashtra ruled the kingdom. Gandhari was happy with her one hundred sons and all was well. But tragedy struck in the springtime, when the leaves were young, when flowers bloomed and birds sang sweetly from the trees. Pandu was overcome with love for his wife Madri, but as he took her hand, the sage's curse struck Pandu and he fell to the ground, dead. Madri began to wail and begged Kunti, 'Let me die, I cannot live without Pandu! Look after my boys, you have always been a better mother than me. I know that you will look after my sons as your own!'

Kunti took Madri's twins, letting their mother die with her beloved husband. Kunti knew that she would never survive in the forest with five little boys and so she gathered the children together and started towards Hastinapura.

Bhishma and Dhritarashtra were upset when they heard about Pandu's death but they welcomed Kunti back warmly, as a daughter of the family. 'Pandu's sons have a right to live here,' said Bhishma. 'He was the king before he decided to spend his life in the forest.' And so it was that Kunti and her sons and the twins born of Madri lived in the palace with Gandhari and Dhritarashtra and the other Kaurava elders.

Pandu's five sons came to be known as the Pandavas and the sons of Dhritarashtra, the king, carried the family name and were called the

Kauravas. The boys grew up together, eating and drinking and sleeping in the same place. But they had no affection for each other. Bhima was the biggest and the strongest of them all and he ate twice as much as everyone else. He took advantage of the strength that he had inherited from his father, the wind, and could often be a bully. Duryodhana, smaller in size but more alert, was arrogant, for he was the son of Hastinapura's king. He hated Bhima with all his heart. He muttered and mumbled against him, but always under his breath, because if Bhima heard him, he was sure to respond with a well-aimed kick or a blow to the chest that would knock Duryodhana to the ground.

Duryodhana plotted against Bhima all the time and once he even gave him food laced with poison. Bhima collapsed after greedily eating all that was placed before him. Duryodhana made his attendants bind his cousin hand and foot and toss him into the river, sure that Bhima would drown and never bother him again. But the poison left Bhima unconscious only for a little while. The cold waters of the river roused him and he broke the bonds that restricted his limbs. He rose to the surface and swore that he would be even more vicious when he wrestled with the Kauravas and when he practised against them with his heavy mace which no one else could even lift.

Bhishma was ageing and he knew that he needed help to raise the one hundred and five rowdy princes in his custody. He asked Kripa, a great archer and learned in all the holy books, to train the boys in the arts of war and kingship.

One day, the princes were playing with a ball which fell into an open well. The well was deep but the boys could see the ball bobbing on the surface of the dark water. They tried as hard as they could to retrieve the ball – Yudhishthira even lost his ring in the process – but to no avail.

They were just about to give up and go back to the palace when a man they had never seen before appeared, as if out of nowhere. His clothes were rough and worn but he had the air of someone who knew that he was out of the ordinary.

'Give me a bow,' said the man. 'I'll bring your ball back.'

'But you have no arrows,' said one of the princes, clutching his quiver protectively.

The stranger smiled and picked up a sharp, pointed blade of grass. He placed it in the bow and released the bowstring. The blade of grass flew into the well. Faster than lightning, faster than the wind, faster than the blink of an eye, the man shot one blade of grass after the other from the bow. He seemed to have ten arms, the bow sang, its string thrummed, the blades of grass hissed as they flew through the air, each one piercing the blade that had been released before it. In seconds, there was a chain of grass. The man pulled the chain of grass towards him. At the end of it was the lost ball, pierced through its centre. Along with it glittered Yudhishthira's ring.

The princes were amazed and they went running to Bhishma, tumbling over their feet and their words in their excitement. 'Grandfather, Pitamaha! We have just met a man who is a magician! He can use his bow and arrows against anyone and win, even against our teacher Kripacharya. He's even better than you, Pitamaha! Come and meet him!'

Bhishma came to where the stranger stood, still and silent, and said, 'Who are you, sir? What has brought you to Hastinapura?'

The stranger looked Bhishma in the eye and said, 'My name is Drona. I am looking for work.'

'And why should I hire you to teach my children?' asked Bhishma. 'You have not bowed to me or honoured me in any way.'

'I don't need to bow to you, Bhishma,' said the man. 'I am born of the great brahmin sage Bharadwaja. I hold the magical weapons of Parashurama, my teacher, in my mind. It is you who should honour me, son of Shantanu!'

Bhishma did not smile but he held out his hand and said, 'Come, Drona. Teach the princes of Hastinapura. Not only how to use their arrows and swords and spears, teach them how to be men of pride. Make them warriors in body and in spirit!'

Drona came to live at the Kaurava court with his wife and child and became the princes' most respected and beloved teacher.

Drona knew that Arjuna would be his greatest student but he tested him constantly. Once, he pointed to a bird sitting in a tree and told

the princes to string their arrows into their bows and take aim. But before they released their arrows, he asked them, one by one, 'Tell me, what do you see?'

Yudhishthira said, 'I see the sky, I see the tree, I see the bird in the tree . . .'

'Stop!' shouted Drona.

Duryodhana said, 'I see the sky is blue, I see the tree is green, I see the dark bird in the branches where the leaves are fresh and young . . .'

'Enough!' cried Drona.

And so it went on, with none of the princes being given permission by Drona to shoot. Then it was Arjuna's turn. 'What do you see, Arjuna?' demanded Drona.

Arjuna pulled back the string of his bow, as far back as it would go, taut and steady. He drew in his breath and said, quietly, 'I see the eye. I see only the eye of the bird.'

'Shoot!' said Drona.

The bird dropped to the ground with its wings still fluttering, its eye pierced by Arjuna's arrow. Drona embraced Arjuna and said, 'You are truly my student! I will make you the greatest archer the world has ever known.'

Drona also taught Arjuna how to fight with a mace and a sword, with lances and spears, and from a chariot. He taught him to take on many men at the same time and shared with him the secrets of the great weapons that he had received from his teacher.

One day, the princes were in the forest, accompanied by their attendants and their hunting dogs. One of the dogs went after an animal's trail and could be heard barking furiously in the distance. The princes followed the sound but it stopped abruptly. In a clearing, they came upon the dog whose mouth had been stitched up with a mesh of arrows so that it could not bark but was otherwise unharmed. They looked around, for they wanted to know who had performed this miraculous feat of archery.

In the shadow of a tree stood a young man, dressed in animal skin, his long hair matted and tied on top of his head, his body glistening like the polished teak wood pillars in the grand public hall of the Kaurava palace. It was clear that he was the archer who had sewn up the dog's mouth with his arrows. The princes asked him who he was and where he had learned to shoot with such skill. He said his name was Ekalavya, that he was a forest dweller. 'I have learned my skills from Drona,' he said modestly.

The next day, the princes asked Drona about Ekalavya. Arjuna was angry. He said to Drona, 'You said that you would make me the greatest archer in the world. And now, there is a boy in the forest who shoots better than me. You promised me that I would have no rival!' Drona was puzzled but he said nothing and went with Arjuna to meet the person who had disturbed his beloved student so much.

When Ekalavya saw Drona, he bent low and touched his feet. He stood with his head bowed and his palms joined.

'I have never seen you before. How can you be my student?' said Drona. 'I am a teacher of kings and princes, I don't teach low-born forest dwellers like you.'

Ekalavya said, 'Master, I watched while you were teaching the Pandava brothers and the Kaurava princes. I made a clay statue of you and, every day, I worshipped it before and after I learned from you. You are my teacher, I have no other. All my skills and prowess, I owe to you.'

'If I am your teacher, where is my fee?' sneered Drona.

Ekalavya said, 'Ask me for anything. I will give you whatever you ask.'

Drona's eyes were steely, his breath was calm. 'Give me your right thumb,' he said.

Ekalavya did not flinch. His sword glinted in his left hand. It swished through the air and even before it had completed its arc Ekalavya's right thumb lay at Drona's feet. Blood from the boy's wounded hand dripped on to the forest floor and was quickly absorbed by the patient earth.

Drona said to Arjuna, 'He will never be able to draw a bow or shoot an arrow without a thumb. I have kept my promise to you.' He turned on his heel and walked away.

Time passed and the princes grew into able warriors. Kripacharya and Drona decided it was time to show the neighbouring kings and the citizens what their royal students had learned. They organised a friendly competition in a large arena and invited people to challenge the young princes. All the Kaurava elders came, and the women, too – Bhishma, Drona and Kripacharya as well as Dhritarashtra and Gandhari, accompanied by Kunti.

There were wrestling matches and duels with the mace. Some spectators noticed that although Bhima was larger and more powerful, it was Duryodhana who was the more agile and skilful. Madri's sons, the twins Nakula and Sahadeva, were unmatched in their handling of horses and bulls. Arjuna won all the archery contests with ease and was also far better than his brothers and cousins in the all-round contests.

Amidst cheers and the stamping of feet and loud clapping, as Arjuna was just about to be declared champion by his teachers, a young man appeared at the entrance to the arena. He shone like the sun, his ears glittered with the earrings that he wore and his entire body seemed to be covered in golden armour. 'Wait!' he said. 'I want to challenge Arjuna!'

The crowd cheered even more loudly as they were enjoying this contest of skills and didn't want it to end. Kunti fainted when she saw the dazzling young man. She had to be revived by her attendants who fanned her with peacock feathers and splashed cool rose water on her face.

'Who are you?' asked Kripa. 'Who is your father, what is your lineage?'

'I am Karna. They call me the charioteer's son,' said the young man, his head held high. 'My parents found me abandoned by the riverbank and made me their own. My teachers are . . .'

Bhima shouted, 'Only street dogs don't know who their fathers are! You can't fight us!'

'This is no place for you,' said Drona. 'You are not worthy to challenge a prince. You say that you are a charioteer's son but we don't even know if you are good enough to groom Arjuna's horses!'

'Only someone with royal blood can challenge Arjuna, the Pandava prince,' said Kripa, more gently. 'Step away, please.'

Karna's brightness dimmed at the shame that had been heaped upon him in public. He was about to walk away from the arena when Duryodhana spoke. 'Stop, Karna! Listen to me, my teachers and elders who are so quick to insult people that they do not know. Is it only the fact that Karna is not a king or a prince that stops him from fighting Arjuna? If that is the case, then here and now, as the son of King Dhritarashtra, I will anoint Karna the king of Anga, the eastern province that I command! Let him fight Arjuna as his equal!'

Karna hesitated. He looked over to where Duryodhana stood. He saw a man handsome and strong in every way, but with a dangerous gleam in his restless eyes. He saw a man whose arms were held wide open and who moved to embrace him.

Karna felt a lump in his throat but he swallowed hard and said, 'But you don't know who I am, either. Why are you doing this, what do you want from me?'

Duryodhana clasped Karna by his strong, wide shoulders and said, 'I believe that we make our own destinies if we are given the chance to do so. I am giving you that chance. All I want in return is your loyalty and your love, nothing more and nothing less. Be my ally, Karna, stay with me even when you doubt me!'

'You have given me the respect that I have craved all my life, Duryodhana. I will never doubt you, I will die for you!' said Karna and he knelt as the sacred waters that made him king of Anga were poured over his head.

'Come, Arjuna!' roared Karna, as he rose from his knees and thumped his chest. 'Come, our destinies await us! Let the world see which one of us is the greater warrior!'

Surya, the sun god, bathed his son in a shaft of light and Karna blazed with all the glory that was rightfully his. Arjuna stepped forward readily, but he was blinded by the rays of the sun that glinted off Karna's natural armour. Karna and Arjuna, brothers who did not know one another, began to fight. They fired arrows that hit their targets that they could not see, their swords slashed through figures made of clay and straw with equal accuracy and swiftness, their chariots rumbled and circled the arena as contest after contest was presented to them. Indra, god of the storm, sent the clouds to shade his son Arjuna when he was tired. He sent cool winds to dry Arjuna's sweat as he panted and heaved against his opponent who matched his every move and manoeuvre.

Kripa and Drona muttered quietly to each other. 'Who is this Karna?' they said. 'He is Arjuna's equal in every way.' 'He's better than Arjuna, we must stop this competition immediately!'

Kripa raised his hand and spoke. 'Enough! We have seen enough! This is the end of the competition, there is no winner!'

The crowd shuffled to its feet and grumbled but Kunti was finally able to raise her head and breathe normally. Duryodhana rejoiced and embraced Karna, for he knew that he had found a friend, a friend who would forever be Arjuna's sworn enemy. Arjuna went back to his brothers, who cheered him loudly, but a shadow had fallen upon his heart. His combat with Karna had affected him deeply and he knew that, in the end, only one of them would survive the deadly rivalry that had just begun.

A Bride for the Brothers

Ugrashravas said:

When he was a boy, Drona lived in the hermitage of the great teacher Bharadwaja where, together with others his own age, he learned the great texts as well as the skills of a warrior. Drona excelled in all that he did and he often helped his friend, Prince Drupada of Panchala. The two were inseparable and swore undying loyalty to each other. Drupada even promised Drona half his kingdom. When their period of study ended, Drupada went back to rule Panchala but Drona, despite his talents and his hard work, remained poor for many years. He was unable to provide for his wife and son and finally, though it shamed him greatly, he decided to ask his friend for help.

Drupada laughed when Drona came to him. 'We say all kinds of things when we are young, you cannot really expect me to hand over half my kingdom to you. A poor brahmin cannot be the king's friend! Go, Drona, find your fortune elsewhere!'

Drona felt deeply humiliated and walked away with his head hanging low. But a burning ember of revenge had lodged inside him and it was to guide his actions in the years that lay ahead.

Drona made himself the greatest teacher of warriors that the world had ever seen. When he had finished training the Pandava and Kaurava princes, he asked for his fee. 'Attack Drupada's kingdom and bring him to me in chains,' he said. It was Arjuna, Drona's best student, who was able to do what his teacher asked. Drona took half Drupada's kingdom and sent him home.

Now it was Drupada's turn to swear revenge against his former friend. He went back to Panchala and, without any delay, he performed a powerful ritual that would give him a son, a son born to kill Drona.

Out of the ritual's sacred fire rose three beautiful children – a daughter as dark as the smoke from the shuddering flames, a handsome young boy and another little girl. And Drupada knew that he only had to wait for his children to grow up for the bitter anger in his heart to dissolve.

Vaishampayana said:

In Hastinapura, Duryodhana's hatred for his cousins grew stronger, like a fire fanned by the wind. Yudhishthira's gentle nature, Bhima's great strength, Arjuna's singled-minded concentration and the physical beauty of the twins had made the sons of Pandu popular with Hastinapura's citizens and Duryodhana burned with anger and jealousy. Despite the finest foods and the softest beds, he could not eat, he could not sleep.

One day, he said to his father, Dhritarashtra, 'You are blind, so you cannot see how your brother's sons are loved by your own people. I am your son, I will be king after you. As long as Pandu's sons live in the city, they will always be my rivals for the throne!'

Dhritarashtra stroked his son's head and said, 'They are like my sons, too. I cannot abandon them. Everyone knows that you are the future king. Why do you worry so much?'

Duryodhana pushed his father's hand away and raised his voice. 'You let Pandu rule in your place. His sons will always believe that they have a right to be kings. And our people will support them. Even Bhishma favours them! Listen to me, father. Send them away, let them do whatever they want far away from here, let our people forget them and turn their attention to me.'

Dhritarashtra loved his nephews and he missed his brother who had always stood by him. But his blood ran cold when he heard Duryodhana's words. He spoke to his counsellors, without revealing what was in his heart. 'Kunti still mourns the death of her husband. A distraction will be good for her. Let us send her and the Pandavas away for a little while. Where should they go, where their hearts will be uplifted?' The counsellors told him about Varnavata, a pleasant city in the north that had an annual fair, filled with bazaars, games and amusements.

Dhritarashtra summoned Kunti and together they made plans for the visit to Varnavata. The Pandavas were excited to get away from

Hastinapura and Duryodhana's relentless hostility towards them. But in the dark rooms at the back of the palace, Duryodhana was meeting other people who listened to his concerns with greater sympathy than his father.

Gandhari's brother, Shakuni, who had come with her when she was married, was cunning and shrewd. He said, 'Nephew, this is our chance to get rid of those five forever. You will never have to worry about them again. Listen, I have a plan. My friend Purochana is a great architect. I will ask him to build a house of lac in the forests close to Varnavata. We will invite Kunti and the Pandavas to stay there. Lac catches fire easily.' He winked. 'There could be an accident – a careless candle, a kitchen fire not fully put out – that would make the whole house go up in flames. Everything in it, including the people who happen to be there, would be turned to ash in minutes!'

Duryodhana's eyes narrowed into slits. He took a deep breath and said, 'Let us talk to Purochana at once.'

On a bright, sunny day, Kunti and the Pandavas said their joyous farewells and set out for Varnavata. Bhima carried his mace and Arjuna his bow and arrows, but they were happy and sensed no danger. They were told that a beautiful house had been created for them by the royal architect outside the city. They could live there even as they enjoyed all the pleasures that Varnavata had to offer. They moved into the house happily, admiring its details and commenting on its comforts.

But back in Hastinapura, Duryodhana's conversation with Shakuni had been overheard. There were many in the palace who remembered the terrifying omens at Duryodhana's birth. They knew that he held the power to destroy his family completely and they watched him carefully as he grew into a noble but discontented man. Swift as the wind but quieter than a baby's breath, messengers were dispatched to Yudhishthira and they told him about the house of lac and about the plot to burn it down while the Pandavas slept. At once, Yudhishthira spoke to Kunti and alerted her to the danger that they were in.

A few days later, Kunti had a plan. Close to them in the forest lived a poor woman who had five sons. 'We will bring her to our house and we will give her and her children fine food to eat and much wine to drink,' Kunti said to Yudhishthira. 'Our enemies will set the house on fire but we will escape through an underground tunnel that is being prepared for us. The woman and her sons will be drunk and full of food, they will sleep through anything. The house will go up in flames and in the morning, when people see the burned bodies of a woman and five young men, they will think that it is us, Kunti and the Pandavas, who have died. But we will be safe. We can live in the forest. No one will look for us because they will be sure that we perished in the fire.'

Everything went exactly as Kunti had planned. The poor woman and her five sons were burned to death when the lac house was set alight while the Pandavas and their mother fled to safety, leaving behind their fine clothes and jewels.

The brothers smeared their bodies with dust and wrapped their bright weapons in bark and leaves as the family moved deeper into the forest and found a suitable place to live. It was by a stream and the trees around the small clearing were thick enough to provide them with shade but not so dense as to cover the sun. They built a hut there and, each day, the Pandava brothers, disguised as brahmins, went into the city to beg for food. If people noticed their strong bodies, wide chests and sturdy arms, they said nothing, but filled their bowls generously with grain.

What the Pandavas did not know was that the forest was inhabited by fearsome rakshasas who stayed hidden all day and became immensely powerful as darkness fell. In the dense trees beyond the clearing where the Pandavas lived lay the domain of Hidimba. He was as large as a mountain, covered with hair and with fangs and claws that could rip apart an elephant with ease. Hidimba loved nothing more than a meal of juicy human flesh, and when he realised that his favourite food was so close, he sent his sister Hidimbi to kill the Pandavas and turn them into a sumptuous meal that they could enjoy together.

Hidimbi moved silently through the shadows, avoiding the moonlight that splashed the forest floor. She approached the Pandavas' little camp. Bhima always slept outside the hut so that he could guard his family at night. The moment she saw that mighty man with his great arms, his strong legs and his chest as broad as a riverbank in summer,

Hidimbi was struck by the arrows of love. Her love was so pure that it changed her from a monstrous creature into a woman of gentle beauty. She crept closer to Bhima, holding her breath so as not to wake him. But Bhima was alert even in his sleep. He woke to find the most beautiful woman he had ever seen leaning over him. In a trice, he had trapped Hidimbi in his arms.

'Who are you, creature of the night?' he whispered harshly. 'Tell me, before I squeeze the breath out of your lovely body!'

Hidimbi trembled and said, 'I am Hidimbi, my brother Hidimba is a rakshasa and he sent me here to capture you, but, Bhima, I have fallen in love with you. I want to be your wife and live with you forever! We must hide! My brother is determined to eat you and your family.'

Bhima smiled. 'Your brother should be afraid of me, not I of him,' he said. 'I cannot take my eyes off you, sweet woman! We can think about your brother later. Let us get to know each other first.'

While Bhima and Hidimbi were enjoying each other's company, Hidimba was getting hungrier and angrier. He charged through the forest towards the Pandava hut, his massive arms and legs crushing plants and destroying low-hanging branches. When he saw his sister with Bhima, he leapt on to Bhima's back with a thunderous roar and wrapped his hands around his neck. Deftly, Bhima flipped the rakshasa over his head and began to pound him with his fists and his feet.

Their battle was fierce – they grunted and growled, they rolled on the ground, they pushed and kicked and pummelled and punched. Kunti and her other sons, who had been awakened by the noise, watched from the side, their hearts thumping with fear. At last, Bhima got the better of Hidimba and smashed his chest, breaking his ribs as easily as if they were matchsticks.

He stood up and wiped the sweat from his face, grinning. He stretched his arms and said, 'I needed that exercise. It's been a while since I had such a good fight!' Then he turned to Hidimbi, who was hiding behind a tree. 'Come,' he said to her. 'Since you plan to be my wife, let me introduce you to my mother!' Hidimbi stepped forward shyly.

Kunti said, 'I can see that you and my son love each other but you know that we need him for our own protection. I cannot let you take him away from us.'

Hidimbi replied, 'Mother, I will take him only for one year and, each day, I will bring him back to you at sunset, before night falls. During the day, I will show him my world and all the pleasures that it holds.' Kunti looked at her son's face which was soft with love and agreed to let him marry the rakshasi.

Hidimbi thanked Kunti and said, 'I will give Bhima a powerful son, a son worthy of the illustrious family to which he belongs. My son will be at his father's side when he is most needed and he will make you all proud.' She took Bhima by the hand and they walked together to where the sun was rising behind the trees.

Soon after, Kunti and the Pandavas moved to a small village called Ekachakra and took shelter with a brahmin family. One day, they awoke to the sound of sobbing and found their brahmin hosts in tears. They told the Pandavas that it was their turn to provide the local rakshasa, Baka, with his meal – all he needed was two buffaloes, a barrel full of rice and a human being.

Bhima laughed and said to the brahmin woman, 'Boil the rice, mother. I'll roast the buffaloes and wait for Baka. I enjoy killing rakshasas!'

Shaking with fear, the woman tried to warn Kunti and Bhima about Baka, his greed and his great might, but Kunti reassured her. 'My son is the equal of any rakshasa. Do not fear for him. He will kill Baka and your village will be safe for all time.'

Bhima carried the barrel of rice over to a clearing and settled down to roast two huge buffaloes. He thought he would wait for Baka to come and claim his meal but, after all those days of eating only what he got in his begging bowl, he could not control his hunger. He fell upon the food with delight.

Meanwhile, Baka had smelt the roasting meat and charged in the direction of the delicious smell. He knew what to expect from his meal – rice, meat and a human being – but when he got there, he saw a rather large young man sitting in front of an empty barrel of rice and the bare bones of two buffaloes. Baka was outraged and attacked the audacious human being who had dared to eat his food.

Bhima was ready for the rakshasa and he stood firm against Baka's blows and punches. Then he suddenly bent low and slipped under Baka's flailing arms. He grabbed the roaring rakshasa around the waist, lifted him over his head and whirled him around in the air. Baka howled and Bhima smashed him to the ground, breaking his body. He dragged it to the village gate and left it there.

When the villagers finally had the courage to emerge from the huts where they were cowering in fear, they were amazed to see the rakshasa dead. The family that the Pandavas lived with said nothing about who had killed the rakshasa and Bhima went back to being a gentle brahmin who ate only what he was given.

One day, while they were begging for food in a town close by, the Pandavas heard about a contest that would win the hand of a beautiful princess. Even though they were still disguised as brahmins, they thought they should try their luck. After all, a new bride would please their mother.

They travelled to Kampilya, where the contest was being held, and when they reached, they realised that the princess was the daughter of King Drupada of Panchala. People said that she was tall and shapely, that her eyes shone like stars in the night sky and her hair was a river of darkness that flowed down her back. Kings and princes from all over had come to win her.

Drupada wanted a special man for his daughter and so he had created an elaborate mechanical wheel that sat on top of a high pole which stood in a shallow pool of water. Above the spoked wheel, which revolved slowly, was a fish that spun in the opposite direction. The men who wished to marry Draupadi had to string the bow they were given and then shoot the fish through the spokes of the revolving wheel. They were not allowed to look up at the fish as they drew their bows. Instead, they had to take aim by watching the wheel and the fish in the reflection that shimmered in the pool at the base of the pole.

King after king and prince after prince tried and failed. Drupada was getting a little anxious, but his son, Dhrishtadyumna, stood firm as the suitors were disqualified, one after the other, determined that his sister would only be given to the best of men.

The Pandavas watched from the stands of the arena, sitting with some brahmins who had been drawn to the spectacle, even though they were not skilled enough to participate in the contest. They saw that Duryodhana and Karna were also there, in the enclosure meant for princes. Arjuna knew that if anyone could pierce the fish, it would be Karna. But he also knew that Drupada would never let his daughter marry the son of a charioteer, no matter what status Karna had earned through his friendship with Duryodhana.

With his shoulder cloth, Arjuna covered the scars from his bowstring that marked his upper arms and stepped forward. 'I will shoot the fish and win the hand of Panchala's princess in marriage,' he said.

A murmur arose from the crowd when they saw his simple clothes, his bare feet and his hair tied in a knot on top of his head. 'He looks like a brahmin! How can he compete for the princess if he is not from a royal family?' someone shouted.

'Yes, yes, throw him out!' shouted another.

Dhrishtadyumna raised his hand for silence. 'This man has a fine, noble face. I do not doubt that he is well born. I declare him worthy of trying to win my sister!' He handed Arjuna the bow that the other suitors had used.

Arjuna strung the unaccustomed bow with ease. It bent to his will like a banana plant in a strong wind. Arjuna could see the fish reflected in the pool as clearly as if it were swimming round the edge of a pond. The spokes of the wheel threw moving shadows on the water that were uneven and irregular. He called to mind all that Drona had taught him. He closed his eyes and calmed his breath. One by one, he concentrated on the parts of his body that he would use to send his arrow to the target – his strong legs, his lower back, his broad chest, his scarred upper arms, his ears that would tell him when the bowstring was ready to be released. He nocked the arrow into the bow and pulled it taut, waiting for it to speak to him. When it did, he opened his eyes. In the instant between pulling in his breath and exhaling, Arjuna knew that the arrow had left the bow. With his mind, he followed it until it had pierced the fish's belly.

The crowd cheered wildly and Arjuna lowered his bow. Across the arena, he saw Panchala's princess. She was smiling as she came towards him with a marriage garland made of flowers and studded with shining gems. But many of the kings present were not at all pleased. 'Stop that brahmin!' they shouted. 'He can't take away a princess!' They leapt over the fence of the royal enclosure with their weapons drawn and ran towards Arjuna. In a trice, Bhima had reached his brother's side. He was armed with an enormous tree trunk and he was striking out in all directions. Quickly, Yudhishthira and the twins joined Bhima and surrounded the princess. Fighting off the other kings and princes, the Pandavas moved swiftly out of the arena as Drupada pacified the angry kings.

Along with his brothers, Arjuna took his prize, Draupadi, for that was her name, back to the village where they lived. Dhrishtadyumna followed them, because he had suspicions about who the five brahmin brothers, with their strong arms and their skill with weapons, really were. When he saw them enter the village of Ekachakra and go to Kunti, he knew that they were the Pandavas. His heart leapt with joy,

for his sister had, in fact, found the right home for her future. He told his father what he had discovered and Drupada sighed. 'It is good that she has been won by a warrior and will live as a queen.'

Kunti was cooking when her sons came home. They stopped at the door to wash their feet and Arjuna called out, 'Look, mother, look what we've brought home today!'

Kunti did not raise her head and replied, 'Whatever it is, my sons, you must enjoy it equally.'

The Pandavas were stunned. 'But . . . but we have come home with the bride that Arjuna won. She is the princess of Panchala!' stammered Yudhishthira.

Kunti came out and looked at the young woman standing there, surrounded by the five men. She burst out, 'O my sons, my sons, what have I said! I cannot take my words back. What will you do now?'

'We will honour your word, mother,' said Yudhishthira and Arjuna nodded in agreement. 'Draupadi shall be a wife to us all.'

Kunti blessed her sons and welcomed Draupadi into her home. 'You will be the daughter I never had and the wife my sons need when trouble comes,' she said, as she kissed the young woman's forehead. She knew that behind her daughter-in-law's luminous beauty, there was a core of steel, tempered in the fire from which she had been born.

The Pandavas Get Their Own Kingdom

Ugrashravas said:

With their appearance at the contest for Draupadi's hand in marriage, news of the Pandavas and Kunti being alive had spread. To some people, that news brought great joy but there were some who fumed with anger. By now, Drupada had invited his sons-in-law and their mother to live with him. Draupadi was happy to leave the small hut behind and be with her family and friends again so the palace rang with her joyous laughter.

But in Hastinapura, the dark clouds of envy and hatred had returned and they cast a long shadow that crept all the way into the grand assembly hall. The elders grew restless and finally Bhishma Pitamaha, the grandfather who had everyone's respect, called a council meeting. With heavy steps, the ministers and advisers of the Kaurava court gathered, for they knew in their hearts that the moment of reckoning had arrived.

Dhritarashtra was helped to the throne by his sons. There was an uncomfortable silence. Bhishma spoke. 'The Pandavas are alive. We should call them back to Hastinapura and make arrangements to divide the kingdom between the sons of Pandu and the sons of Dhritarashtra. Dhritarashtra and Pandu are both my nephews. They ruled our lands together and I love them equally.'

Duryodhana leapt up from his seat. 'I see no reason to give up any part of my father's kingdom to the Pandavas. Their father went to live in the forest, that's all that they deserve to inherit!'

Karna also stood up. He said loudly, 'Why do you always take their side, Bhishma? This throne belongs to Dhritarashtra and his sons, not to those homeless wanderers who share one wife between them!'

Bhishma ignored him and said to Duryodhana, 'It will do you good to remember that Yudhishthira is older than you, Duryodhana. He has more right to the Kaurava throne than you do. What I am suggesting will let you be king, too.'

Bhishma looked around the room but no one had the courage to catch his eye. Except Drona, who spoke up fiercely. 'Honourable Bhishma has shown us the way forward. Bring the Pandavas back to Hastinapura! It is the duty of this royal court to divide the kingdom between the sons of those who have ruled it wisely and well until now.'

Duryodhana and Karna continued to mutter to each other and their discontent was visible to everyone in the room. Vidura, wise counsellor to the king, was a gentle man who never raised his voice but was heard by everyone. 'If we do not give the Pandavas their rightful share of the kingdom, we will have war, a war between brothers that will destroy us all. We must not forget the ill omens that appeared at Duryodhana's birth and the prophecy that came with them. We cannot allow his arrogance to end the glorious reign of the Kauravas. The Pandavas are now the sons-in-law of Drupada, who is rich and powerful. They will have arms and allies, we cannot hope to defeat them in battle. Listen to Bhishma. Share the kingdom with Pandu's sons!'

Dhritarashtra trembled as fear gripped his heart. He knew what Vidura said was true, that his sons were no match for the Pandava warriors and their friends. He could not bear the thought of his beloved children dying on the battlefield but he also wanted his own sons to rule after him. He said, 'Go, Vidura. Bring my brother's sons back to their home with all honour. Take clothes and jewels, horses and chariots. Let them return to Hastinapura as the princes that they are.' But there was no joy in his voice when he spoke.

The next morning, Vidura set off for Kampilya. When he reached Drupada's city, he was pleased to see that Krishna, the Yadava prince, was already there with his brother Balarama. Krishna was a cousin to the Pandavas, for his father was Kunti's brother. He knew them all, but he loved Arjuna best and would do anything to ensure that he was happy and secure. Balarama had a special affection for Bhima who had been his student – he had taught the big, heavy man to wield a mace with deadly force. But it was Krishna who was known and respected the world over. He was a formidable warrior and a very capable adviser. There was also something else about him that made people wary – his dark skin shone with a divine radiance, his eyes blazed, and though no one had ever heard him laugh, he always seemed to be smiling.

When Krishna heard that Dhritarashtra planned to divide his kingdom between his sons and the Pandavas, he advised Yudhishthira to return to Hastinapura and accept the offer. Kunti was worried that her sons would once again be vulnerable to Duryodhana's harassment and murderous intentions but Krishna said, 'Have no fear, dear aunt, I shall be with your sons always and I will protect them. You know that Arjuna is like my second self, I will never let him be harmed.'

The Pandavas returned to Hastinapura. They were warmly received by the elders who showered their new bride with affection, but Duryodhana muttered darkly and stayed away from the celebrations. Dhritarashtra announced that he would give the Pandavas the land around Khandavaprastha, the ancient city that had fallen into ruin. There, they could build a new city and rule as their forefathers had in the past. But Khandava was harsh and barren. Breezes searched among the rocks and stones, and because they had no flowers or plants to caress, they whistled through the roofless palace and fallen pillars of the abandoned city and whipped up the brown dust that covered the dry ground.

As the Pandavas considered building their new city in that wasteland, they continued to live in the Kaurava palace. They abided by the rules they had made for themselves such that each of them could enjoy the company of the wife they shared. When the brothers had married Draupadi, they had made a pact that none would interrupt the other when it was his time with their common wife – if he did, he would have to go on a pilgrimage and stay away from the family for a whole year. One day, Arjuna walked into Yudhishthira's chamber when he was with Draupadi, playing a game. Arjuna froze when he saw them together, laughing quietly as they teased each other about who was winning. Yudhishthira sensed Arjuna's presence, but before he could even greet his brother, Arjuna bowed low and said, 'I have broken our agreement by entering your chambers so thoughtlessly, brother, I must go away for a year. Give me your blessings.'

Draupadi leapt up from her seat. 'Arjuna, you made a mistake. You did not enter our room intentionally! This is not the time for you to leave us, we need you here!' she cried.

Yudhishthira reached out and held her arm. 'He must go, dear wife of ours. He must honour the pact we made when we married you,' he said calmly. 'When he returns, he will bring back much that we will value and be grateful for.' Yudhishthira turned to Arjuna and said, 'Go well. Keep us in your heart and do not lose track of our situation.'

Arjuna understood what his brother was saying. With the unequal division of the Kaurava kingdom and Duryodhana's seething discontent, he knew that one day there would be a war, a war between cousins that would be unlike any war before. He knew that he must make alliances with kings who would send their armies to fight on the side of the Pandavas. One way to ensure the loyalty of their allies was to marry into their families. Arjuna sighed deeply when he thought about how Draupadi would react to the new wives that he would bring back with him. He turned resolutely in the direction of Dwarka, Krishna's city.

Krishna told Arjuna that his sister, Subhadra, had always loved him but that Balarama had promised her to Duryodhana. Krishna had seen a shadow of sadness fall across her face when she was told the news of her betrothal to a man she did not like. Krishna wanted Arjuna to kidnap her and take her away. 'You know that among warriors kidnapping a woman is not a crime if you marry her. I cannot bear to see my sister unhappy, Arjuna. I will help you take her away from Dwarka. She will be a good wife to you and she will bear you a magnificent son!'

Krishna and Arjuna decided that the best time to take Subhadra was at a festival that was coming up. In the midst of all the merriment and commotion, Krishna drove the chariot as Arjuna swooped past the women, grabbed Subhadra by the waist and lifted her up beside him. Subhadra smiled at Arjuna even as they were chased by Balarama and his angry men. Krishna took them to safety and then persuaded Balarama to consent to the new wedding plans.

When Arjuna returned to his family after a year, he saw that Yudhishthira had grown disheartened with the wilderness that had been given to him as a kingdom. But Krishna promised the Pandavas that they would build a city that would be envied in all the three worlds. First, they would have to clear the ancient forest that occupied part of the land, a forest dense with trees and creepers and home to different kinds of animals and birds who had lived there for many generations.

As Krishna and Arjuna were thinking about how to deal with the forest, they saw a tall, thin man walking towards them. 'I am hungry,' he said simply. 'Will you feed me?' Arjuna and Krishna readily agreed to give him whatever he wanted to eat. The man seemed to grow taller and his eyes shone brightly. He said, 'I am Agni, the god of fire. Burn down this forest for me. The trees and animals will satisfy my hunger. A snake named Takshaka lives there, he is Indra's friend. Each time I try to devour this forest, Indra sends the rain to put out my flames so that Takshaka will not lose his home. I will give you the weapons you need to keep the flames alive till I am no longer hungry.'

Arjuna bowed and Agni gave him Gandiva, the celestial bow that was equal to a thousand bows and he taught the young warrior the secret words that would empower it. He also gave him a quiver of arrows that would never be empty as well as a chariot drawn by four white horses, swift as the wind and who could outrun every other horse in the land.

Agni entered the forest and it began to blaze. The flames rose higher than the tallest trees and the crackle of the burning wood was as loud as the rumble of thunder. Smoke filled the air and ash was carried far and wide by the wind. Indra saw the flames and sent his mightiest rain clouds to douse the fire. But Arjuna and Krishna had begun to circle the forest in their chariot, shooting arrows into the air so fast that they formed a net over the trees and stopped the rain that Indra had sent.

The forest burned and burned, and as Agni satisfied his hunger, he cared nothing for the animals that lived there. With their wives and children, they tried to escape the inferno, but Arjuna's chariot drove them back into the flames. Indra searched for his friend Takshaka, the great serpent, but he could not see him anywhere. He hoped that Takshaka was somewhere else, safe from the flames that had trapped his family and were destroying his home.

The fire burned for days, long after Agni had gone back to the realm of the gods. When it finally died down and there was nothing left but a scorched earth, Krishna said, 'This is where the Pandavas should build their new home. Maya, the architect of the gods, is a friend of mine. He shall make a palace for you, the likes of which has never been seen by human eyes!'

Maya came swiftly when he was summoned and, in no time at all, the most marvellous palace arose before the eyes of the astonished Pandavas. It shimmered in the light, its pillars seemed not to touch the ground, its vast halls were draped in soft silks and rich brocades. Fountains tinkled and their delicate spray cooled the air, clear pools in open courtyards mirrored the sky and sweet fragrances wafted through the rooms. Draupadi was delighted and clapped her hands with glee. Yudhishthira agreed to begin the many rituals that would establish his kingship without delay.

Kings great and small from neighbouring lands were all invited to the grand rajasuya sacrifice that was planned and soon the new palace was buzzing with activity as priests gathered and altars were built and entertainments were organised. 'Your new city shall be called Indraprastha,' said Krishna. 'Invite your cousins here for a few days. Let them enjoy your hospitality and spare no expense for their comfort.'

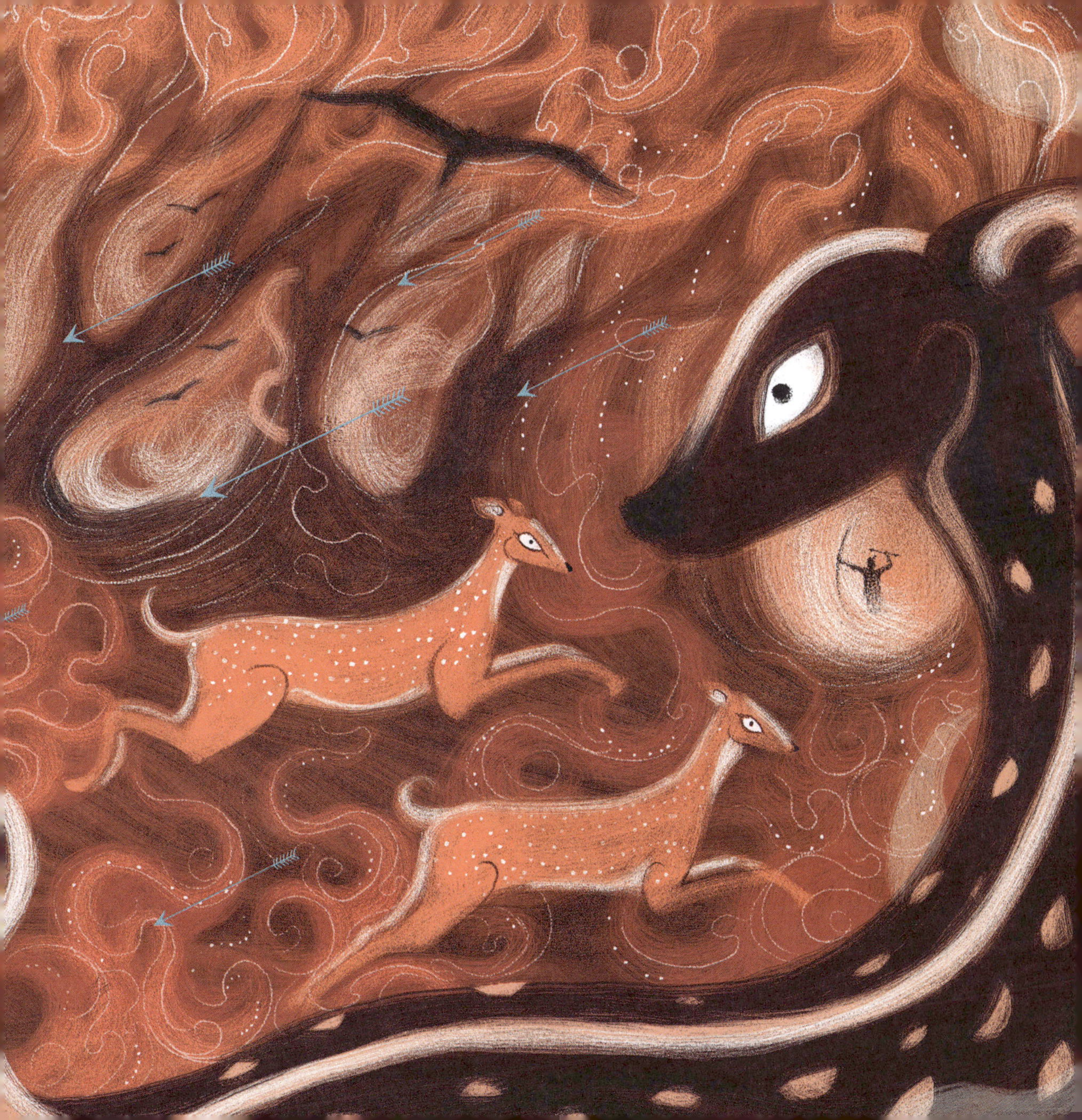

The royal entourage from Hastinapura came to share in the happiness of the Pandavas and to celebrate a new beginning in their family relationship. They were amazed when they saw the beautiful palace. Bhishma embraced the brothers one by one and kissed their foreheads as he blessed them. Drona could not stop smiling as he clapped Arjuna, his favourite student, on the back. Gandhari's maids described the marvels of the palace to her in whispers and Vidura guided Dhritarashtra by the hand to a comfortable seat. But Duryodhana brought anger and envy with him and Karna, too, was not willing to appreciate the new lives the Pandavas had made for themselves.

Duryodhana saw Yudhishthira, magnificent on his golden throne and surrounded by kings. He saw the beautiful women that lived in the palace and could not help but admire slim-waisted, dark-skinned Draupadi who was adorned with flowers and jewels. His mouth twisted in a bitter smile as he walked around the palace. He saw a pool in front of him and lifted his garment to keep it from getting wet. But it was only a crystal floor that gleamed like sunlit water. Duryodhana pretended that nothing had happened and walked over to the next enclosure where he saw rare blue lotuses blooming in a tranquil indoor pond. He looked carefully and decided that this was another polished floor that only looked like a pool. He stepped firmly forward only to find his feet wet and the hem of his gold-bordered garment splashed with water. 'Look!' he heard Draupadi say. 'The blind son of a blind king!' Laughter echoed through the halls as the visitors and courtiers mocked Duryodhana.

'I will have my revenge,' muttered Duryodhana as Karna led him away.

The Dice Game

Ugrashravas said:

As Yudhishthira's grand rajasuya sacrifice commenced, the elders and kings gathered to participate in the coronation and acknowledge Yudhishthira as the greatest king of them all. After the ceremonies were over, Yudhishthira turned to Bhishma and said quietly, 'Grandfather, there are so many kings here, so many men who are worthy of respect. They all command wealth and large armies, they have been with us in the past and they will surely be with us in the future. They are our teachers, our family, our friends and our allies. Whom should I treat as the most honoured guest of them all? Whose feet should be washed first?'

With no hesitation at all, Bhishma said, 'Honour Krishna first, he is the greatest of all the kings and princes gathered here, he is greater even than the elders. He is your most important friend and adviser.'

Yudhishthira told Sahadeva to wash Krishna's feet. Whatever he might have been thinking, Sahadeva betrayed no surprise and did as he was told. The assembly of kings applauded but a thick, loud voice rang out above the cheering. 'Why is Krishna being honoured before everyone else? This is a gathering of kings and warriors, he is just a cowherd!' shouted a king named Shishupala.

A stunned silence followed Shishupala's outburst, but before anyone could say anything, a discus flashed through the air and Shishupala's head fell to the ground with a thud. 'I have forgiven him one hundred insults, as I had promised long ago,' said Krishna, his voice like ice. 'This is one more than that.'

Krishna pledged himself to the Pandavas and began to advise them regularly about diplomacy and matters of state. He also never let them forget that a war with their cousins was certain and that they needed as many friends and allies as they could gather. On a previous occasion, he had urged Bhima to kill Jarasandha, ruler of Magadha, a rich and powerful kingdom in the eastern regions. Jarasandha had captured one hundred kings and kept them imprisoned so that he could sacrifice them to Shiva.

'The kings you rescue will be in your debt forever, they will help you fight the Kauravas. Jarasandha is an old enemy of my family's and we have never been able to defeat him,' Krishna said. 'By getting rid of him, you will also be doing me a favour. You know I will return that a hundredfold, when the times comes.'

Bhima had torn Jarasandha's body in half, as if it were made of paper.

Vaishampayana said:

Duryodhana returned from the Pandavas' palace in a foul mood and shut himself away with Karna. He refused to meet his family or perform any of his royal duties. Everyone knew that he was enraged at having been laughed at and that he had sworn revenge, but no one was willing to approach him and restore him to good humour.

Except one man, wily Shakuni, who stayed hidden in the shadows of the court. He entered Duryodhana's chambers and said, 'Nephew, why this long face, these eyes red with anger, these restless steps, these long, deep sighs as if the world has ended? Come here, listen to my plan that will give you everything you want. And more.' Shakuni placed his arm around Duryodhana's shoulders and led him away from the windows.

'Invite Yudhishthira to a dice game. He is addicted to gambling and he is a very poor player. Get him to stake his kingdom and we can win it from him,' said Shakuni.

'But a dice game is about luck,' said Duryodhana doubtfully. 'How can you be sure we'll win?'

'Because I am master of the dice,' said Shakuni with a wicked smile. 'The dice obey me, they fall as I command. And I shall play instead of you. We can win anything! Everything!'

Duryodhana was still not convinced. 'But if he's a bad gambler and always loses, why would he accept an invitation to play with us?'

Shakuni's eyes gleamed. 'A dice game is part of the rajasuya rituals. By custom, Yudhishthira cannot refuse this invitation. Besides, his love for the game will bring him here like a moth to a flame! You will have your revenge, my man, you will have far more than you ever dreamed of. Don't delay, send the invitation to Indraprastha today!'

Despite the misgivings of his brothers, Yudhishthira accepted Duryodhana's invitation to the dice game. 'Shakuni is going to play for Duryodhana,' sputtered Bhima. 'You know he cheats at dice and no one can stop him. Don't play, brother, we beg you!'

'I can't refuse,' said Yudhishthira, not meeting his brother's eyes. 'I am the king, I must play.'

'We will come with you,' said Arjuna quietly.

Together with Draupadi and Kunti, the Pandavas reached the Kaurava court. Draupadi went to the women's apartments, but Kunti joined Gandhari and the male elders in the grand assembly hall where the dice game had been arranged. They were all there – blind Dhritarashtra, venerable Bhishma, fierce Drona, loyal Kripa, gentle Vidura and many of Duryodhana's ninety-nine brothers. Karna was there, too. Shakuni was already rolling the dice between his fingers impatiently. The Pandavas honoured their uncle and teachers and bowed before Grandfather Bhishma. Bhishma stroked Yudhishthira's hair and said softly, 'Play wisely, my son. May the gods be with you.'

Yudhishthira, Duryodhana and Shakuni seated themselves in the centre of the assembly hall and the others gathered around to watch. The four Pandava brothers sat behind Yudhishthira, as if to protect him.

'What will you stake, Yudhishthira, king of Indraprastha?' said Shakuni, smiling widely, as he handed the dice over so that his opponent could play first.

'I stake a hundred thousand gold coins contained in chests of silver,' Yudhishthira said and rolled the dice as Duryodhana matched his stake.

'I have won,' said Shakuni, when the dice fell in his favour.

'I stake a thousand handsome men and a thousand beautiful women who work in my palace,' said Yudhishthira.

'I have won,' said Shakuni, picking up the dice.

'I stake my massive, well-trained war elephants and my chariot horses, white as snow and swift as the wind – I have thousands of them, I stake them all!' said Yudhishthira, his hand trembling slightly as he played.

'I have won,' said Shakuni.

The silence in the assembly hall was deafening. No one moved, all eyes were fixed on the dice as they continued to favour Shakuni, even as Yudhishthira made higher and higher stakes and lost all that he bet, leaving his treasury and his palace empty.

'I stake my priceless necklace, made from pearls that emerged when the gods churned the ocean,' said Yudhishthira, 'and all the jewels that my brothers and I are wearing!'

But Shakuni won.

'I stake my kingdom,' cried Yudhishthira desperately.

Someone in the grand assembly called out a warning, but it was too late. Duryodhana and his brothers and Karna slapped each other on the back and laughed and clapped as Shakuni tossed the dice triumphantly in the air. He had won, again.

'I stake my brothers,' shouted Yudhishthira. 'Stout-hearted Bhima who fights with the mace, Arjuna, the best archer in the world, and Madri's sons, the twins with the golden eyes!'

'Come here,' Duryodhana laughed, when Yudhishthira lost his brothers. 'You belong to us now!'

'I stake myself!' cried Yudhishthira, unable to stop himself. He hung his head when he, too, was lost.

'I have nothing more to stake,' he said quietly. 'Everything I have is now yours. The game is over.'

The Kaurava brothers started to cheer and gather up the jewels that the Pandavas had lost and placed on the ground where they had been sitting. But Shakuni held up his hand and stopped them.

'You have one more thing to stake, Yudhishthira, son of Kunti,' he said. 'If you stake that and win, we will give everything back. Are you willing?'

Yudhishthira did not raise his head. 'I have nothing,' he said.

'You have Draupadi, your common wife. Stake her!' Shakuni smiled slyly.

Yudhishthira looked up as if in a daze.

Bhima could bear it no longer and he roared, 'Shame, brother, shame! Stop! Stop this terrible game that has turned us into beggars and looted our honour!' Arjuna and the twins held him back as he charged towards Yudhishthira who seemed no longer in control of himself.

'Draupadi,' Yudhishthira said quietly and his eyes filled with tears. 'There is no woman as beautiful as her. She is tall and slim, her hair is a river of darkness that falls down her back all the way to her knees, her eyes are the shape of lotus petals and they shine brighter than the stars, her skin is softer than the finest silk. Yes, I stake Draupadi, the finest woman in the three worlds!'

The Kaurava brothers could not contain their glee when Draupadi was also lost. But Bhishma groaned and buried his face in his hands. Dhritarashtra asked his attendants what had happened for he could hear the tumult in the hall, Kunti clutched Gandhari's hand, Vidura wiped the sweat from his forehead and Drona stared unseeingly into the distance.

'Dushasana!' Duryodhana summoned his brother. 'Go and bring Draupadi here. She is now our slave, she doesn't need to be in the women's chambers!'

Dushasana rushed into the women's section of the palace and found Draupadi. 'You are called to the assembly, woman! Come with me!' he snarled.

'Speak to me with respect,' Draupadi replied. 'I am a queen and I am your sister-in-law!'

'You're not a queen, you're a slave! Your virtuous husband, the son of Dharma, has gambled you away. You belong to the Kauravas, even your husbands are now slaves. We can treat you as we please! Hurry up,' he said, as he pushed her forward.

Draupadi could not believe what she was hearing, but she was fearless and she spoke with steel in her voice. 'I cannot come into the assembly. I am not dressed for the public, I have my period and my garment is stained. Go back and tell the kings and the elders that I am not available to them!'

Dushasana laughed. 'You have no choice, Draupadi, you cannot refuse your masters. Come!' and he grabbed her by her hair, that river of darkness that snaked down her back. Draupadi kicked and screamed but Dushasana dragged her through the corridors and into the hall of the Kauravas. He pushed her and she fell, landing hard on the floor. When she raised her head, her eyes were blazing. She looked at Yudhishthira and said, 'Husband, is it true that you lost me in a game of dice, that you gambled me away like an object that you cared nothing for?'

Then she turned to the elders, to Bhishma and Dhritarashtra and Drona and Vidura and Kripa. She said, 'And you, men who are honoured, who are respected for their virtue and their good deeds, you kings who protect your citizens, you let this happen? You have allowed a woman of your house, a royal woman, to be brought into public when she is not meant to be seen! Shame on you and shame on this family!'

She turned her gaze to Duryodhana and Karna. Duryodhana patted his thigh and said, 'Come and sit here, my pretty!'

Draupadi's voice was steady. She said, 'You have insulted me, Duryodhana. You do not know what you have unleashed!'

Draupadi said to Bhishma, 'Tell me, grandfather, did Yudhishthira lose me before he lost himself? If he had already become a slave, what right does he have over me, how can he gamble me away when he owns nothing, not even his wife!'

Bhishma said, 'You are right, daughter–'

But Duryodhana interrupted him and said roughly, 'Enough,

Draupadi, wife to many men! No one is interested in what you think! Dushasana, she doesn't like what she's wearing, so take off her clothes!'

Dushasana lunged towards Draupadi and started to pull at her stained garment. Draupadi stood still. She placed her palms together and raised her hands above her head. She closed her eyes and called on the gods to protect her. Dushasana pulled at her clothes. He pulled and he pulled. The more he pulled, the longer her garment became, its cloth piling up on the floor. Endless yards of cloth billowed around the room, flowing like water, swirling like whirlpools in an angry river, rising like the waves of the ocean when the tide rushes to the shore. Some people say they saw Krishna standing in the shadows behind Draupadi. The river of cloth that covered her seemed to be flowing out of his body.

Dushasana gave up and fell among the cascading folds, holding his head.

Bhima shouted, 'I will kill you, Dushasana. I will break open your chest and I will drink your blood. And you, Duryodhana, I will smash that thigh of yours, that one that you are so proud of!'

Draupadi opened her eyes. She looked at Dushasana and said, 'I will wear my hair untied until the day I can wash it in your blood!'

Dhritarashtra finally spoke. 'This has gone too far. Daughter, I will grant you whatever you want. Tell me what I can do for you.'

'Release my husbands from their slavery,' she replied.

'It is done. Ask me for something more.'

'This is enough, lord of the Kauravas,' Draupadi said. 'Let us leave this place with honour.'

'I return to Yudhishthira everything that he has lost,' said the old king, his voice shaking. 'I give him back his kingdom, his wealth, his brothers, everything.' Duryodhana and Karna began to protest but they were silenced by a look from Bhishma.

Duryodhana let the Pandavas and Draupadi start their journey back to Indraprastha and then he ran to his father and said, 'What have you done, father! We had defeated them completely without using a single weapon. Call them back! Let us have one more game. One throw only. The winner will rule this undivided kingdom and the one who loses will live in exile, in the forest, for twelve years. A thirteenth year will be spent among people, but in disguise. If they are discovered, the whole period of exile begins again!'

Dhritarashtra hesitated. He loved his son more than anything in the world and could not bear his unhappiness and his anger. He sighed and his heart was heavy. 'Call the Pandavas back,' he said to his retainers.

The Pandavas returned for Yudhishthira to play one last throw. Again, Shakuni rolled the dice, again he won. The Pandavas and Draupadi went into exile, leaving Kunti in Dhritarashtra's palace.

The Exile

Ugrashravas said:

The Pandavas and Draupadi settled in the forest but it was not a happy time. Draupadi was angry because her husbands had done nothing to protect her from the Kauravas. She was uncomfortable in the forest, fearful for their safety and displeased with their small hut, the poor food and all the other discomforts she had to face. Yudhishthira spent his time talking to sages about the meaning of life, Arjuna was away for long periods, collecting weapons for the war, the twins lived their own lives and so it was only Bhima who noticed that

Draupadi's eyes had lost their sparkle, that her steps were heavy and that her mouth was often set in a grim and unhappy line.

One day, he found Draupadi sitting alone, caressing a beautiful flower. 'Look, Bhima,' she said. 'Isn't this the most gorgeous flower you have ever seen? And this fragrance, it's like something from the realm of the gods!'

'Where did you get it?' asked Bhima. 'If it makes you so happy, I'll bring you more!'

'I think the wind brought it here,' she said. 'I can still smell its traces in the air.'

'I won't return until I've found more like it.' Bhima kissed her gently and set off into the deep forest, moving quickly through the trees, following the flower's lingering fragrance.

Bhima went further and further. The trees grew closer together and the forest grew darker. Vines as thick as a man's arm twisted themselves around tree trunks and the ground was covered with dense undergrowth. But there seemed to be sunlight in the distance and Bhima moved towards it with determination.

Soon, a narrow path appeared and as Bhima hurried along, his mace at his shoulder, he tripped. He examined the ground closely – an animal's tail lay across the path. Bhima tried to kick the tail away but failed to move it. He looked around and saw an enormous monkey sleeping under a tree in a shaft of sunlight that turned his fur to gold. The monkey was old and he breathed heavily as he slept with his head on his giant arms that had obviously once been strong and powerful.

'Hey monkey!' shouted Bhima. 'Get your big fat tail out of my way!'

There was no response from the monkey. Bhima prodded him with his mace and leaned over to yell in his ear.

The monkey opened one eye. 'Why are you disturbing the sleep of the old? I am tired, can't you see? Let me sleep! You look like a warrior, you're so big and strong. You move my tail,' he said and made himself comfortable again.

'Monkey, your tail is moth-eaten and scraggly. But it suits you, you ragged old creature. Your head is balding, too, and your beard has turned white. Moving your tail is nothing for me! I am the son of Vayu, I can leap over you the way Hanuman leapt over the ocean!'

The monkey smiled. Bhima put both his arms around the massive tail and heaved. The tail did not move. Bhima rested his foot against a rock and steadied himself and tried again. The tail remained exactly where it was. Bhima thrust his mace under it and strained. Nothing.

Bhima was panting. He wiped the sweat off his forehead and said, 'Who are you, monkey? You are no ordinary creature. I am sorry for my arrogance. Bless me!'

'I am Hanuman. In another age, I helped Rama rescue his wife,' said the monkey. 'I, too, am the son of Vayu, god of the wind. I am your brother!'

Bhima wept tears of joy as he beheld Hanuman, famous in all the three worlds. 'Show me your great form, brother, the one you took to leap over the ocean!'

'I will do this for no one but you,' said the monkey sweetly. And he began to expand. His chest filled out, his arms and legs rippled with muscles, his tail swayed tall over his head, its tuft flashing in the sunlight. Bhima fell to his knees in wonder. Hanuman lifted him and embraced him. Bhima felt a new energy surge through his limbs and his tiredness melted away. 'Stay with me,' he said. 'Be always by my side!'

'You will not see me, but I'm with you at all times,' said Hanuman gently. 'I will appear on the battle banner of the Pandavas, so you know that I'm there. Now go on your way – the flowers you seek lie ahead, in Kubera's garden. May you be successful in all that you do!'

Bhima fought a fierce battle with Kubera's attendants to get the flowers which he then carried carefully back to Draupadi. She placed them in her hair and strung them together to wear around her neck and on her wrists and, for a little while, the old sparkle that Bhima loved returned to her eyes.

Vaishampayana said:

In the forest, Yudhishthira was the least unhappy of all the brothers. He enjoyed the quiet life, away from the tensions and duties of the court. He had always been a man of peace, reluctant even to argue with anyone, and truly believed that when they returned to their city after being away for thirteen years, all would be well and that he and the Kauravas would rule separately with no hostility between them.

Even though the sage Vyasa came to visit and warned him that his cousins were preparing for war, Yudhishthira thought about all the ways in which peace could be established for the benefit of everyone. Draupadi did not hide her feelings and often told Yudhishthira that he was being short-sighted and foolish, that he should be angry at what had been done to her, that he should see war as inevitable and as a way to restore their lost honour. Yudhishthira would smile and continue his conversations with the wise men.

But Arjuna thought differently and began to use this time away from prying eyes to gather as many divine and magical weapons as he could. He travelled to the far corners of the earth, close to where the gods lived, in his search. He went to the frozen north and, in order to persuade the gods to give him what he needed, he performed the most severe of all penances.

He started by eating only the withered leaves that fell to the ground and, each month, he ate less and less until he was living on nothing but air. He stood on the toes of one foot, his arms raised above his head, his eyes closed in meditation.

The gods are nervous when humans disturb the three worlds with their ascetic practices. And so, Indra, the king of the gods, sent a group of beautiful dancers from his court to distract Arjuna. Led by Urvashi, the most beautiful of them all and Indra's favourite, they gathered around the lone warrior. Their bangles and anklets tinkled, their voices were light and melodious as they called to him and asked for his attention. Arjuna did not waver. He stood as still as if he had been carved out of stone.

Finally, Urvashi grew angry and said, 'Arjuna, you have ignored us, and in doing so, you have insulted us. I curse you – that you will have to live among women for a whole year of your life. You will be like them and no one will know you for the great warrior that you are!'

Spring came and Arjuna relaxed his austerities. As he opened his eyes, he saw a wild boar charging towards him. Arjuna picked up Gandiva, the magnificent bow he had received from Agni, and fitted it with a single arrow that always found its mark. He released the arrow and the boar fell heavily to the ground, bleeding. Arjuna ran to the animal and saw that another arrow had also pierced the boar, right next to his own.

A man dressed in deerskin stood over the boar, a bow on his shoulder. 'This is my prize,' he said. 'It is my arrow that killed the boar!'

'No,' said Arjuna, looking the hunter in the eye. 'It's my arrow that killed him. The boar is mine.'

'Aha!' said the hunter. 'You're a better marksman than me, are you? Let's see whose arrows are swifter and more accurate!'

Arjuna loosed a volley of arrows that sang through the air. His hands moved like lightning and the twang of the great Gandiva echoed in the mountains. But he saw that the hunter had not moved or flinched or ducked. In fact, he was laughing. He had caught Arjuna's arrows in his hands and between his teeth and he slowly rotated himself on one foot. As he turned, Arjuna saw that the man before him was Shiva, the three-eyed lord of animals, destroyer of the worlds.

'I am impressed with you. You are a great archer!' said Shiva.

Arjuna knelt and said, 'Shiva, if I have pleased you, give me the weapons I need to fight Bhishma and Drona and that pretender Karna! Give them to me so that I can be victorious in battle!'

Shiva said, 'I will give you my favourite weapon, son of Indra. I will give you the Pashupata, no one is invulnerable to that. Use it wisely – if you use it against a foe who is not worthy, it can destroy the worlds!' Shiva summoned the deadly weapon and bestowed it on Arjuna, along with the power to call it when it was needed. And then he vanished.

In Hastinapura, the Kauravas were also taking advantage of the absence of their rivals. Karna knew that Arjuna was arming himself and that, in the end, they would fight each other to the death. He said to Duryodhana, 'Let me leave the city and go in search of weapons, weapons that will help us defeat the Pandavas. I know Arjuna is not in the forest with his family, I know he is asking the gods to favour him. I must do the same, we must be prepared for war in the best possible way.'

Duryodhana said, 'Go, my friend. Come back when you are ready, when your weapons are a match for your great courage and your skill.'

Karna went in search of Parashurama, who held many magical weapons that he gave only to his best students. Parashurama was known for hating all kshatriyas, for they had deceived his father and killed him. Parashurama was not a forgiving man and his temper was as well known as his formidable fighting skills.

Karna approached Parashurama, who was now an old man living by himself, far from everyone and everything. 'I want to be your student,' said Karna, bowing before the legendary teacher. 'I want to learn everything you know.'

'Are you a kshatriya, a warrior by birth?' asked Parashurama, frowning.

'No, I am Karna, I am a charioteer's son,' said Karna truthfully.

'You have to live with me and look after me for as long as it takes for you to master what I know. The better you are as a student, the more I will teach you,' said the old man, studying Karna from head to foot. 'Are you ready for this – you will have to cook my food and massage my limbs, you will have to fetch water and watch over me when I sleep.'

'Yes,' said Karna. 'You are my only teacher. I surrender to you.'

Karna cared for Parashurama the way he would have cared for his own father and, in return, Parashurama taught him more and more, impressed with Karna's skills and dedication. He even gave him the secret of the brahmastra, the most destructive weapon that the world has ever known, and cautioned him that all weapons must be used with care and that some weapons could be used only once.

One day, Parashurama was tired and lay down to rest. It was a hot afternoon and Karna placed his teacher's head in his lap and shaded him with his body so that he could sleep with ease. Suddenly, Karna felt an intense pain in his thigh, a pain like he had never felt before, as if something were tearing through his skin and chewing on his flesh. He looked down and saw that an insect was boring through his thigh which was now oozing blood. Karna stiffened, he held his breath, he bit his lip, he did everything he could to stop from screaming in pain. Parashurama stirred. 'What is this wetness?' he said, wiping his face. He saw blood on his hand. 'Blood!' he shouted. 'Are you injured?'

Karna looked down at the hideous insect that was eating his flesh. He groaned. Parashurama stood up, shaking with anger. 'You lied to me, you are a kshatriya!' he said. 'Only a kshatriya would not react, would suffer pain like this in silence. Leave here immediately, Karna! I curse you! I curse you to forget all that I have taught you, the magic words that will bring you the deadliest weapons. You will forget them when you need them most!'

Karna begged and pleaded and apologised but all Parashurama would say was, 'Get out! Get out of my sight before I kill you myself!' Karna walked away sadly, knowing that he was now vulnerable in battle.

Finally, the twelve long years that the Pandavas had to spend in the forest ended. There was only one more hurdle before they could reclaim their kingdom. Vyasa came to see them again. 'This is the most difficult of all your years in exile. You must leave the forest and spend a year among people, but in disguise. Have you thought about where you will go and how you will live?' he asked Yudhishthira.

'We have heard that King Virata is a good man. He also hates our cousins. We can hide in his kingdom for this year,' replied Yudhishthira. 'But we haven't talked about our disguise yet. Who shall we be, what shall we do?'

'Think about this well,' said Vyasa. 'This year will make all the difference to your future.'

Yudhishthira said, 'Let us present ourselves to the king as servants who are looking for work. We can say that we worked with the Pandavas and that we are well trained and well mannered. I will say that I have been Yudhishthira's companion, that we have played dice together and talked about matters of life and death.'

Bhima said, 'I will be a cook! I love food, so this will be easy for me!'

'I will offer myself as a dance teacher to the young princesses,' said Arjuna. 'I will dress as a woman and act like one.' The others laughed when he said that.

'How will you hide your strong arms and your scars from your bowstring?' asked Bhima. But Arjuna knew that he would be fulfilling Urvashi's curse of living among women for a year and he did not react to the laughter of his brothers or think about another disguise.

The twins said they would look after the king's horses and cows, for they were skilled in the care of animals.

'I shall be the queen's hairdresser,' said Draupadi quietly.

'We must be careful not to make contact with each other or be seen in each other's company,' warned Yudhishthira. 'Duryodhana and his men will be looking for five men and one woman who live and work together. Once we enter Virata's kingdom, we must be strangers to one another.'

Draupadi suppressed a shiver of fear that ran down her spine at the thought of being separated from her husbands. She knew that there was no other way for them to live through their last year of exile but she was afraid, nonetheless. 'I will make it known that I have five gandharva husbands who will come to my rescue if anything happens to me,' she said resolutely. 'Everyone fears these celestial beings who make beautiful music but are also known for their fighting skills. No one will come near me if they know I am protected by them.'

'The king may hate Duryodhana but we don't know about the people around him,' warned Yudhishthira as they set off. 'The Kauravas will do everything they can to harm us so we must remain cautious and watchful.'

Just before they entered Virata's city, Arjuna took his beloved weapons and collected those of his brothers. He wrapped them all carefully in animal skins and hid them in the branches of a large shami tree that grew at a little distance from the road. He bowed and asked the tree to protect their weapons for the last year of their exile and to keep them safe for the war that was to come.

The Kingdom of Virata

Ugrashravas said:

Karna had known both the limitations of the poverty into which he was born and the benefits of the great generosity that he had received from Duryodhana. He was a noble man and took a vow that he would never refuse anything that he was asked for – rather, he would give it with an open heart and with no regrets.

Son of Surya, Karna was born with golden earrings and his body was covered in armour that was the colour of the morning sun. It gave him a natural protection from arrows and other weapons that could pierce his skin. As long as he had the armour, he was safe, hard to defeat in battle and a formidable opponent. The three worlds knew that Karna and Arjuna had been born to fight each other. The decisive conflict in the war that would destroy everything would be between these brothers who did not know who the other really was.

Indra, father of Arjuna, feared for his son's life. He decided to take advantage of Karna's vow and make him vulnerable. One day, he took on the form of a poor brahmin and approached Karna. He said, 'Will you give me alms, young man?'

'I have taken a vow to give whatever anyone asks for. Tell me, what do you want?' replied Karna.

'Give me your golden earrings and this shining armour that covers your body!' said the brahmin.

Without a moment's hesitation, Karna cut off the ornaments that hung from his ears and tore off the armour that protected him. And then he remembered a dream that had recently disturbed his sleep, so he said, 'Wait, brahmin. I was told that this moment would come, when I would be asked to give away the divine protection that I am born with. I know that you are Indra and that you have come to protect my mortal enemy, your son, Arjuna. But give me something in return, something that will make death wait for me just a little longer. Give me the Shakti weapon!'

Moved by Karna's nobility, Indra said, 'Take it, Karna, it is yours alone. No one else has it. But you can use it only once and only against one person. I give you also my blessings, I can bless you with everything except a long life!'

Karna accepted the weapon and Indra vanished.

Vaishampayana said:

When they reached Virata's city, the Pandavas met the king, who was happy to take them on as his retainers when he learned that they had worked in the palace of Indraprastha. 'I hope you are a better gambler than your old master,' he joked with Yudhishthira. Bhima was sent to the kitchen and the twins went to the stables. Arjuna was introduced to the princesses as their new teacher and he danced a little to show them how graceful he was.

The queen, Sudeshna, looked at Draupadi and said, 'Where have you

come from? You don't look like a hairdresser, I don't think you have worked a single day in your entire life!'

Draupadi kept her eyes on the ground and said, 'My husbands are gandharvas, my lady, that is the only unusual thing about me.'

'Very well,' said the queen. 'As long as you know how to care for me, I shall not be concerned about your origins or your family.'

Soon, the Pandavas had settled into a new routine. Draupadi longed to meet her husbands. She knew that Bhima kept an eye on her, for he would often slip her something delicious that he had prepared in the kitchen. Even though the end of their exile was in sight, the months passed slowly for Draupadi. She saw Arjuna every now and then in the women's apartments and that made her happy. But she also knew that the queen did not trust her completely and was watching her carefully.

Bhima's cheerful nature kept him happy in the kitchen as he tried out more and more new dishes to please the king. Yudhishthira was an amiable companion and he kept the king entertained. In the care of the twins, Nakula and Sahadeva, the royal horses and cows had never been healthier. All in all, the king was very pleased with his new retainers and his good humour spread cheer all around.

Every now and then, news from Hastinapura would trickle through the palace and the Pandavas would listen carefully to what was said about the Kauravas preparing for war. They shared news as often as they could but were very careful not to be seen together.

One day, Queen Sudeshna's brother, Kichaka, came to visit the kingdom. He was a famous general and was well known for his success in commanding a large army. Kichaka was also good friends with King Virata who counted on his military skills for his own army and so he was welcomed warmly with much feasting and many celebrations. He would walk in and out of the women's apartments as he pleased when he wanted to see his sister and his niece and, while he was there, he would take a good look at all the serving women who tried not to attract his attention in any way. But Kichaka's eye fell on Draupadi, who stood tall and proud even as she tended to the queen and her daughter. He took every chance he got to be close to her, he tried to speak to her and once he grabbed her hand as she walked by him. Draupadi ignored him and stayed as far from him as she could.

‘Who is that new woman?’ Kichaka asked Sudeshna. ‘She is very beautiful. And also very haughty. Where did you find her?’

Sudeshna replied, ‘She’s very mysterious and I have no idea who she is and where she’s from. I suspect she has royal blood.’ With a smile she added, ‘But you should stay away from her. She says she has five gandharvas for husbands.’

Kichaka guffawed with laughter. ‘Gandharvas! Five husbands! Come on, sister, surely you don’t believe that? Tell her I want to see her tonight. In my chambers!’ he said as he walked away.

Sudeshna knew that Draupadi would not do as Kichaka wanted. So she sent for her and said, ‘From now on, you will take my brother’s meal to him and wait in his room until he finishes eating. Make sure you serve him well.’ Draupadi shuddered, knowing that she could not disobey the queen. She took Kichaka his meal and was careful not to look at him as she placed the food before him.

‘Come and sit here,’ Kichaka smiled. ‘Eat with me, it will make the food all the more delicious.’ He patted the cushions next to him. Draupadi left the room as quickly as she could but Kichaka’s mocking laughter followed her and she heard him say, 'If not tonight, then some other night, my dear! You will be my guest very soon!'

Draupadi ran to the kitchens, hoping to find Bhima. She was in luck as Bhima had stepped outside just as she got there. 'Bhima, help me!' she cried. 'The king's brother-in-law wants me to stay with him in his chambers. I will kill myself if he touches me, I swear I will!'

'I will not let anyone lay a hand on you,' Bhima comforted her. 'Tell him that you have changed your mind, that you will meet him. Come to fetch his meal and I will go in your place. He will never bother you again!'

The next evening, in Kichaka's chambers, Draupadi was a little more friendly. When Kichaka asked her to sit next to him, she forced a smile and said, 'I will spend the evening with you tomorrow. I have not oiled my body with sweet perfumes today, but I will, for you. I shall wash my hair and adorn myself with flowers before I come to you.' Kichaka patted her on the shoulder, saying, 'I'll be waiting!'

Kichaka was in a good mood all of the next day. He hummed and whistled as he wandered through the palace and was unusually kind to his retainers. Evening came and he waited eagerly for his meal to arrive. A heavily veiled figure, smelling sweet and accompanied by the tinkling of anklet bells, appeared with a tray.

'Ah, you're being shy today, I see,' said Kichaka. 'Never mind, we have all night.' He stroked the arm of the person holding the tray. 'I didn't realise that you have such strong muscles. Must be all that work you do all day. Let me see your face,' he said as he tugged at the veil. In a flash, Bhima was upon him, punching and kicking. Kichaka fought back instinctively, pushing against the huge man who was attacking him, biting the hand that covered his mouth. But Bhima had the advantage and he was also very angry. He twisted Kichaka's neck and pushed his head down between his shoulders. He smashed his arms and legs and left his body in a broken heap on the floor.

The next morning, there was pandemonium in the palace when Kichaka was found dead. Sudeshna wept and summoned Draupadi, asking if her gandharva husbands had killed the king's general. Draupadi said nothing but Sudeshna took her silence as confirmation that her husbands were Kichaka's killers. Worried that these celestial beings had reacted so badly when Draupadi had not even been harmed, she told her husband not to pursue the matter of Kichaka's death.

But the king had his own worries. 'Who will lead my army now that Kichaka is dead?' he wondered.

Yudhishthira quietly said, 'You need have no fear, sir. I, too, am skilled in managing an army. I can help you.'

The king was not satisfied but he had no option and so he prayed that his enemies would not use this chance to attack his kingdom.

Meanwhile, as the news of Kichaka's killing spread, Duryodhana grew excited. 'Only Bhima could have killed Kichaka in that manner,' he said. 'This means that the Pandavas are hiding in Virata's kingdom. There are only a few weeks of their exile left, we must expose them immediately!'

Shakuni, who had now become Duryodhana's main adviser, said, 'Let us attack Virata. He has lost the commander of his army and the Pandavas will have to come out and fight if the kingdom is threatened. They will be easy to identify on the battlefield and we can send them back into exile for another twelve years!'

Bhishma and Drona were deeply disturbed. 'Give Yudhishthira his kingdom, put an end to this useless rivalry and hatred,' they said. Duryodhana would not listen, he had set his mind on destroying the Pandavas sooner rather than later and by any means necessary.

Virata was greatly agitated when the Kauravas and their allies attacked his kingdom. 'I knew this would happen. That Duryodhana and his uncle Shakuni!' He turned to Yudhishthira. 'You said you would help me, that you know how to command an army. This is the moment – show me what you can do!'

'The men I came with from Yudhishthira's court are skilled warriors – that cook and the two who look after your animals. Call them into service!'

From the women's quarters, Arjuna watched in disbelief as his brothers were called up for Virata's army. 'They know that I am the best warrior among us all,' he grumbled under his breath. But he, too, knew that the end of the exile was a few days away, and if he were to appear on the battlefield with Gandiva in his hands, he would be identified in a second and their exile would begin all over again.

Duryodhana had been clever – he had pulled the Pandavas out of the city to fight an army of his allies. His own army, led by Bhishma with Drona and Kripa by his side, came around Virata's kingdom and attacked from the other side, pretending that this was not an act of war, but simply a raid on Virata's fabled herds of cattle. The news of the attack reached the palace but there was no one there to receive it. Except Arjuna. He did not waste a minute and went quickly to where Virata's young son was. 'Prince,' he said, 'we have no time to waste. You have to fight back against those who are pretending to be cattle raiders. Don't look so frightened, I will be with you.'

'But . . . but, you are my sister's dance teacher, you are not even a man, let alone a warrior!' stuttered the terrified prince. 'You are sure to have me killed!'

'Trust me,' said Arjuna. 'You don't have a choice – your father's kingdom is about to fall to his enemies.'

Arjuna dragged the reluctant young man with him to where the chariots were and drove quickly to the shami tree where he had left his weapons. He thanked the tree for its protection. He kissed Gandiva, holding the bow close, as if it were a long-lost friend. He thrust himself into a breastplate and tossed the reins of the chariot to the astounded prince who was standing there with his mouth open. 'I am Arjuna, the Pandava,' he said simply and then he blew his great battle conch.

Bhishma and Drona heard the conch and they knew that Arjuna was coming into battle. In the distance, they could see his battle banner fluttering, the one which carried the emblem of a roaring monkey – Hanuman. They heard the unmistakable twang of Gandiva, a bow that sounded like no other. They were pleased but Duryodhana tensed in his chariot until he remembered that he could still send the Pandavas back into exile.

'Grandfather,' he hailed Bhishma. 'The Pandavas have been found during their year of living in disguise. Let us defeat them quickly and put an end to this idea that they will get their kingdom back. They can go back to the forest where they belong!'

'The thirteenth year ended a few weeks ago, Duryodhana,' said Bhishma, his eyes flashing. 'Your astrologers' calculations have been wrong all along. The Pandavas are safe, they have fulfilled the terms of the exile.'

Karna was standing close and he said boldly, 'How can we trust you as the commander of our army when you so clearly favour the Pandavas!'

Bhishma's look would have stopped any other man's heart, but Karna wheeled his chariot around and sped off, raising clouds of dust behind him.

Arjuna knew that he had to first protect the cattle that were being stolen. He drove through the soldiers who had been sent to steal the cows which were lowing pitifully. His rain of arrows scattered the men, and once Arjuna was sure that the cows were safe, he turned to the battle with his true enemies. He told Virata's son to drive directly towards Duryodhana who was unable to withstand the speed and accuracy of Arjuna's arrows. Duryodhana withdrew from the battle, as did Karna whose heart was burning with anger.

When Bhishma and Drona saw that Duryodhana was no longer being attacked on the battlefield, they pulled back, acknowledging Arjuna's skills as a warrior and delighted that the years in the forest had not diminished them. As Arjuna and the young prince drove back to the city after returning the weapons to their hiding place, Arjuna said, 'You cannot tell anyone who I am. That must remain between you and me until my brother Yudhishthira decides that we can declare ourselves.'

In the city, meanwhile, Virata had returned, flushed with victory over the Kaurava allies. He was told everything that had happened in his absence – the cattle raid, the second assault by the mighty Kaurava army, how the dance teacher had taken his young son into battle and how the attacking army had turned back. Virata rejoiced and said, 'Well, that dance teacher could not have done much, so this victory belongs to my son!'

Yudhishthira corrected him gently saying that the credit for the victory should surely go to the dance teacher since the prince was young and inexperienced. Virata lost his temper and threw the dice that he was holding at Yudhishthira, refusing to believe that his son was not responsible for the retreat of the Kauravas. The dice struck Yudhishthira on the forehead and he began to bleed, but before the blood could fall to the ground, he collected it in his cupped hands.

Draupadi ran forward and wiped his head gently with the edge of her garment. Virata watched in consternation and Draupadi said, 'If a single drop of his blood had touched the ground, your kingdom would not have seen rain for a whole year!' Virata's confusion was not lessened by her explanation and he began to wonder who his retainers really were.

Just then, the prince burst into the room and saw Yudhishthira's injury which had been caused by his father. 'Father, you do not know who these people are!' he cried. 'We are safe because of them!'

Arjuna realised that the moment to reveal their true identities had arrived. 'We are the Pandavas. That man, whom you have treated as your servant, is Yudhishthira, king of kings. I am Arjuna and these are our brothers Bhima, Nakula and Sahadeva. The woman who has been with your wife as her hairdresser for this past year is Draupadi, the princess of Panchala.'

Yudhishthira spoke. 'We have lived safely in your kingdom for the last year of our exile and we thank you for all that you have done for us.'

Virata interrupted and touched his forehead to the ground before Yudhishthira. 'It is I who must thank you,' he said gravely. 'My kingdom is safe because of you, my son is alive because of your brother. Let me show my gratitude by giving my daughter Uttara to Arjuna in marriage.'

Arjuna smiled and said, 'She has been like my daughter when I was her teacher. Let her marry Abhimanyu, my son from Subhadra, who is Krishna's sister. He is a good boy and he is the same age as her.'

Abhimanyu and his mother and uncles were brought from Dwarka and the young couple's wedding was celebrated with much joy. With this marriage, the Pandavas knew they had one more powerful monarch on their side.

A Time of Alliances

Ugrashravas said:

Long ago, Bhishma had kidnapped three princesses for his half-brother Vichitravirya, the son of his father Shantanu and his second wife, Satyavati. The eldest princess, Amba, had begged Bhishma to let her go, for she was in love with Shalva, who had promised to marry her. Bhishma saw the tears in her large eyes and gave her permission to leave.

But when Amba went back to Shalva, he said he could not love her any more. 'You have been with Bhishma. He is the greatest warrior the world has ever known. What will I do if he claims you again? I cannot fight him, not even with my entire army. I will not take you back, Amba!' Shalva left Amba without looking back.

Amba's heart broke but she knew of Bhishma's reputation for being honourable and so she decided to go to him for refuge. Surely he would accept her, now that she had been rejected by the man she loved.

This time, however, Bhishma regarded her coldly. 'There is no place for you here. My brother married your sisters and I have taken a vow never to be with a woman. The world is open to you, Amba, go where you will.' Amba could not believe her ears, but like Shalva, Bhishma, too, turned away from her.

Amba's despair turned to anger and she vowed that she would avenge the insult to her. She said, 'Look at me, Bhishma, look at me carefully. Remember me, for I shall return as your death!' She left the city and walked from kingdom to kingdom, trying to find a warrior who would challenge Bhishma to fight. No one would, not even mighty Parashurama. Amba realised that she was alone, that there was not a single man who would help her take revenge on the person who had turned her into a homeless wanderer.

Undaunted, she disappeared into the countryside and started to practise the severe austerities which she knew would eventually bring the gods to her side. First she stood in the fast flowing waters of the river Yamuna, living on nothing but air, uncaring of the heat, the rain and the cold. Then she went into the forest and stood on the tips of her toes for years, eating only half of a leaf that had fallen to the ground.

Word of her practice spread and the sages and ascetics grew worried. But finally, Shiva appeared before Amba and asked her what she wanted. 'I want to be reborn as a man so that I can kill Bhishma,' she said firmly. Shiva said that she would have to be reborn as a woman if she wanted her wish to be fulfilled but that she could retain the memory of her past life.

Amba agreed. She built a funeral pyre for herself and, without a second thought, jumped into it, ending the life that had brought her only shame and suffering.

Meanwhile, Drupada was performing powerful rituals for the birth of children. Out of the sacrificial fire rose Draupadi, dark as smoke, and her radiant brother Dhrishtadyumna. And along with them came another beautiful baby girl. Drupada's heart went out to the child immediately and he picked her up in his arms. He named her Shikhandi for there was a knot of hair on top of her head. She was brought up along with both Draupadi and Dhrishtadyumna. Shikhandi's interest lay in the arts of war that her brother was being taught and soon her family got used to thinking of her as a boy.

One day, Shikhandi found a garland of blue lotuses hanging on the city gate. She placed it around her neck and ran to show her father. Drupada shuddered. The garland had stayed on the gate, unclaimed for so many years, because it was said that whoever wore the garland would kill mighty Bhishma.

Vaishampayana said:

Duryodhana could not believe that the Pandavas had successfully completed their period of exile and that his father's advisers were suggesting that their kingdom be returned to them. 'We will not give them even five villages!' he snarled in the great assembly hall and stalked off to his own apartments.

The Kauravas had been gathering allies while the Pandavas were away and they had made many friends. It was now the turn of the Pandavas to do the same and messengers flew back and forth to all the great kings who had not joined the Kauravas.

The Pandavas were restless. Bhima grunted and growled all day as he practised with his mace, Arjuna fingered the scars on his arms and shoulders and polished his weapons, the twins made sure that the horses that would be yoked to the battle chariots were exercised every day and were fed and watered generously. And Draupadi waited, her hair unbound, her eyes red with anger.

Yudhishthira knew that whatever Bhishma, Drona, Kripa and the other mighty warriors who lived at Dhritarashtra's court felt in their hearts, loyalty would mean that they fought on the side of the Kauravas. He said to his brothers, 'The greatest fighters will be arrayed against us when this war begins. The Kauravas have also negotiated for large armies and food and weapons for their soldiers. We are at a disadvantage already. Arjuna, Krishna loves you more than anyone else in the world. Ask him to fight on our side, ask him to pledge the

Yadava armies to us. Go to Dwarka without delay. I will feel secure if I know that Krishna is with us – there is something about him that makes him unlike any other man on earth.'

Arjuna set off at once, racing against the wind, to reach his friend as soon as he could. But Duryodhana's spies made sure that Duryodhana, too, rushed to Dwarka to talk to Krishna. Krishna was asleep when the cousins reached his city. They were asked to wait beside his bed. Duryodhana lunged for the seat made of gold and covered with soft silks that stood at the head of Krishna's bed but Arjuna sat at Krishna's feet.

A little later, Krishna awoke. He smiled and said, 'I know why you are here. But before you ask me for anything, you should know that I will not fight, I will not carry arms. You can choose either my armies with their experienced warriors and all their weapons or you can choose me, alone.' He paused. 'Because I saw Arjuna first, as I opened my eyes, I will let him make the first choice.'

Arjuna said simply, 'I choose you, Krishna!'

Duryodhana could not believe his good luck. He jumped up from his seat and shouted for joy. 'Hah! I will take your armies, Krishna, I will take your soldiers and their weapons and your horses and elephants and chariots and all that you offer me!' He could not wait to go back to Hastinapura with his news. He was now sure that the Kauravas would win the war. 'What use is Krishna if he isn't going to fight,' thought Duryodhana.

As soldiers gathered and the rumbling of battle chariots and elephants and horses filled the air around Hastinapura, Krishna felt that he had to make one more attempt at peace, a chance to avoid a war that he knew would kill everyone and signal the end of an age. It would leave the earth barren and burned, women would be widowed and children would be orphaned, darkness would enter people's hearts and it would be a long time before the sounds of laughter and singing would be heard again. He had to make an effort to prevent this.

Krishna arrived at the Kaurava court and was greeted with courtesy but not with joy. Faces were grim and there was tension in the air. He knew the elders did not want the war but he also knew that war was the only thing that would satisfy Duryodhana who was confident that he would destroy the Pandavas once and for all. Karna stood by him, as did his brothers and his uncle, Shakuni.

Blind Dhritarashtra wanted only his son's happiness, and though Gandhari spoke firmly to her husband and her sons about a chance for peace, they were not listening. Their ears were already filled with battle cries and shouts of victory. Duryodhana was losing patience with all those that opposed him and, in his delusion, he made a plan to detain Krishna when he arrived at the palace and keep him prisoner.

Satyaki, Krishna's cousin, overheard these plans. He ran to Krishna who was already in the assembly hall and whispered to him urgently. A smile played on Krishna's lips. He looked at Duryodhana and said quietly, 'You don't know me, prince of the Kauravas. You have no idea who I am!' Krishna grew larger and larger and his radiance filled the room. He held all the gods within his body – there was Brahma on his forehead and Shiva on his chest, Agni stood in his mouth, there were Indra and Varuna and the guardians of the four quarters, and there, too, were all the minor deities of the sun and the storm – the adityas, the rudras, the maruts, the vasus and the Ashwins. The divine sages were there and so were the Pandavas themselves.

In the many arms that emerged from his body, Krishna held Vishnu's favourite weapons, his discus, his sword and his mace. Krishna shone, his eyes blazed and his body thrummed with the vibration of the universe. In the great hall of the Kauravas, only Bhishma, Drona and Vidura saw Krishna as he truly was, for he had given them divine sight for this moment. Then, just as quickly, Krishna came back to his normal self. He said nothing but walked out of the hall, leaving behind a stunned silence.

Krishna understood that there was one last thing he could do to try and stop the war. He went to meet Karna. Karna was surprised to see him but he remained polite even though he knew that whatever Krishna had come for was not something that would set his mind at ease.

Krishna sat beside Karna and took his hand. 'What I am about to say will disturb you, Karna, but you must know this before you fight,' he said gently.

Karna looked into Krishna's eyes that were filled with tenderness and compassion. His heart beat faster, but he could not look away and he could not withdraw his hand that Krishna held.

'Kunti is your mother, Karna,' said Krishna softly. 'The Pandavas are your brothers. Do not fight against them.'

Karna shook off Krishna's hand as he rose from his seat. 'Radha is my mother, my father's name is Adiratha, he is a chariot driver,' he said. 'Duryodhana lifted me up in public before a thousand eyes and made me his friend. This is my family, Krishna, I know no other.'

'Listen to me,' said Krishna. 'Kunti had you when she was a young girl, she was frightened, she left you by the river. Like her other sons, you, too, come from the gods. Surya, the sun, is your father. Join the Pandavas! The Kauravas have no chance if you and Arjuna are on the same side, they will surrender. You can stop a war that will change everything that we know, everything that we believe in, everything that makes us who we are. If you fight on the side of the Kauravas, brother will kill brother, student will kill teacher, we will kill our own children! Think, Karna, you can stop this from happening.'

'I cannot betray Duryodhana,' said Karna calmly. 'As for Kunti, I owe her nothing. She abandoned me and now her other sons hate me. Arjuna has sworn to kill me. I will not fight on the Pandavas' side. Go away, Krishna. There are some things more important than saving one's own life. I know fate is against me in this war. But I will fight every day as if victory will be ours.'

Filled with admiration for Karna, Krishna went to meet the Pandavas to help them prepare for the war. But he did not tell them about their eldest brother, for he knew that Yudhishthira would surrender his kingship to Kunti's firstborn son.

Now that all his attempts at making peace had failed, Krishna had to control the war and make sure that he got the result he wanted. He told Kunti, though, about his meeting with Karna and held her in his arms while she wept for the radiant son that she had lost. Krishna said, 'Meet him once before the war begins, Kunti. He worships the sun every day by the river. Go to him, ask him to forgive you. A mother's love can move mountains.'

Kunti waited for Karna on the riverbank. From afar, she watched her eldest son worship the father he had not known. The sun bathed Karna in his glorious light and Kunti's heart overflowed with love. She approached him quietly. Karna was surprised to see Kunti but he was even more surprised at the emotions that flooded his body. He felt tears in his eyes, but he gathered himself and said politely, 'Greetings, good lady.'

Kunti said, 'You are so cold to me. I know that I am the mother of your enemies, but I have something to ask of you. I have heard that Karna gives everything that he is asked for.'

'Speak, madam. If it is in my power to give, I shall,' he said. 'You say I am cold to you and yet there is a feeling within me that I cannot describe, something that I have felt only in my dreams. It is a tenderness, it is the memory of a caress filled with love. I see a woman in my dreams but her face is always covered . . .'

Kunti burst out, 'That woman is me, Karna. I am your mother! The love I cannot give you in our daily lives is what I shower upon you in your dreams! The Pandavas are your brothers . . . come to them with me!' She reached out and touched his arm.

Karna recoiled as if he had been stung. 'Don't touch me!' he cried. 'I cannot bear this – to feel love for the woman who abandoned me when I was a baby! I cannot give you what you ask for, forgive me. I cannot fight on the same side as my brothers.'

'Please, Karna, let me finally have all my sons together!'

'Your sons!' Karna sneered. 'I promise you this, Kunti. I will not kill the twins, the sons of Madri, I will not kill Bhima, son of the wind, I will not kill Yudhishthira, son of Dharma. But Arjuna and I, we will fight to the death. I know that he has already picked the arrow that he thinks will pierce my breast. And I know which of my divine weapons I have chosen for him. I will kill him, Kunti. That way, when the war is over, mother, you will still have five sons!' Karna walked away quickly and he let the tears that he had been holding back flow down his cheeks.

War

Ugrashravas said:

dharmakshetre kurukshetre samavetah yuyutsavah
mamakah pandavascha kima kurvata, sanjaya

Blind Dhritarashtra addressed Sanjaya with these words, asking, 'On the field of the Kurus, on the battlefield of righteousness, they are gathered, eager to fight – my sons and the sons of Pandu – what are they doing, Sanjaya?' In the palace that was cold and dark and silent, they sat together, waiting for the battle that would destroy the Kaurava clan to begin.

Sanjaya, who was Dhritarashtra's charioteer, had been given divine vision for the duration of the war by Vyasa. Like the gods, he would be able to see what was happening in every corner of the battlefield and he was appointed to report all that he saw to the blind king. Sanjaya had sworn to be neutral, to say only what he saw and not what he felt, but he knew where his master's loyalties lay. How could a father not wish for the success of his sons, how could a king not want victory for his own army?

Sanjaya began to speak. 'Mighty armies have gathered at Kurukshetra, some on the side of the Pandavas and others allied with Duryodhana. They are led by the greatest fighters the world has ever known. On your side stand Bhishma, Drona, Kripa and Kritavarma, who leads the Yadava forces. On the other side, there is Yudhishthira, Bhima, the sons of Madri, and Arjuna, the archer who can fire his arrows with both hands. Krishna is his charioteer and has brought Arjuna's chariot to stand between the opposing armies. He waits for Arjuna to blow his conch and signal the start of the battle. But wait, Arjuna has laid down Gandiva, the bow that was given to him by the gods, and he is speaking to Krishna with tears in his eyes.

'Arjuna says, "Krishna, my legs are trembling, my palms are sweating, Gandiva has slipped from my grasp. An unknown fear has gripped my heart. I cannot fight."

'Krishna says, "Stand up, Arjuna! Don't be a coward. This is the most important moment of your life, you have waited for this, you have trained for this, this is what you were put on earth to do. Fight, Arjuna! Pick up your bow!"

'Arjuna says, "I can't, Krishna. How can I raise arms against my elders, my teachers, my uncles, my brothers? I have grown up with these people, they have made me who I am. Let them win the war even before it has started, I care nothing for kingdoms or wealth or victory if they come at the cost of killing my elders and my family. Drive the chariot back, Krishna, I will not fight."

'Krishna replies, "You are a warrior, Arjuna, it is your duty to fight, no matter who stands before you. Each of us must do what we are born to do, we each have our duties, our responsibilities and our obligations, no matter if we are warriors or priests or farmers or merchants. A stable society, a stable world, a stable universe depends on the performance of these duties and obligations. Pick up your bow, Arjuna, prepare to fulfil your obligations to yourself and your family. Do your duty as a warrior and fight in the war that will keep the world safe!"

'But Arjuna does not move. He stands downcast, his proud head with its jewelled crown hangs low, his arms are limp by his sides.

'Krishna speaks again. "Arjuna, all men are born to die and to be reborn. Only I am beyond birth and death, I am eternal, everything begins and ends in me. Have faith in me, Arjuna, and learn to act without being attached to the fruits of your actions. Act freely and in good faith, be steady in your intentions. If you do your duty, you will always be doing the right thing."

'Arjuna says, "But Krishna, how do I know what is true action and how do I develop firm intentions?"

'Krishna says, "There are many different ways to the truth. Listen carefully and I will guide you. There is the way of knowledge, which is through reading the ancient texts and discussing what they say with wise men who will show you the way. There is the way of action, which, as I said, means that you act with detachment, with no expectation for reward. But more than all of these, there is the way of devotion – surrender your actions to me. I will carry the burden of your actions and I will love you and look after you."

'Arjuna says, "Krishna, I am confused. Help me understand this."

'Krishna says, "Look at me, Arjuna. I will show you my true self."

'Krishna expands in size and seems to cover the sky. A great light shines forth from his body. Brighter than the light of a thousand suns, Krishna stands before Arjuna who is almost blinded by Krishna's radiance. He sees all the gods in Krishna's body, he sees the entire cosmos, he sees thousands upon thousands of warriors pouring into Krishna's mouth and being devoured, he sees fire, he sees earth, he sees water, he sees even air.

'Arjuna falls to his knees and whispers, "Who are you, Krishna, what am I seeing?"

'Krishna says, "I am Time grown old, Arjuna, I am the universe, everything exists in me and I am in everything. It is because I love you best that I have let you see me as I truly am. But in a moment, I will be your charioteer again and you will forget what you have seen!"

'Arjuna blinks and sees Krishna standing next to him, a smile playing on his lips. "Come to me, Arjuna!" Krishna says. "Give yourself to me, for I am the only reality there is!"

'Arjuna feels a great calm descend upon him. His breath is steady, his legs and arms are strong, his eyes are clear. He rises and blows his conch, Panchajanya. The war between the Pandavas and the Kauravas has begun, your majesty. And the conversation between Arjuna and Krishna that you just listened to is the Bhagavad Gita, "The Song of God".'

Vaishampayana said:

On the night before the war began, the commanders of the opposing armies met to decide on the rules by which they would fight. Together, they agreed that there would be no fighting before sunrise and all battles would stop at sunset, no one would attack an injured warrior, a warrior who was unarmed or a warrior who had surrendered. A warrior fighting alone was not to be attacked by many, a warrior was not to be attacked from the back, personal combat and duels could only be between warriors who fought with the same weapons, all rules regarding combat with those weapons would be respected, no person or animal not taking part in the war could be harmed. Those brave men did not know this then, but every single one of these rules would be broken in the eighteen days to come, as the war would rage on towards its terrible end.

Before the Pandavas left the great hall of the Kauravas, Yudhishthira laid down his arms and went to his teachers, one by one. He went to Bhishma, Drona and Kripa. He bowed before them and touched their feet. To each one he said, 'Give me permission to kill you and may it be that I do not have to do so.'

Bhishma wiped the tears from his eyes and blessed Yudhishthira, kissing his forehead. Drona said, 'It is good you have said this, Yudhishthira, son of Dharma, or you would have been my first target,' but his eyes, too, were wet and his voice was choked when he spoke. Kripa raised Yudhishthira up and said, 'I will have to fight at my best against you and your brothers but my thoughts will be for your victory.'

Bhishma was the commander-in-chief of the Kaurava forces and he called his men together so that they could plan strategies and manoeuvres. He assigned them all roles and ensured that they would be matched against enemy warriors who were their equals. Bhishma knew the truth about Karna's birth and he decided to do everything he could to keep him away from fighting Arjuna, his brother. He appointed Karna to a lower rank so that the chance of him facing Arjuna was almost impossible.

Karna was incensed. He rose to his feet and said, 'Bhishma, I am tired of your insults. How can you assign me this rank, fit only for a young and inexperienced soldier? I am a skilled archer and swordsman, my spears and lances never miss their mark, I am an expert charioteer as well! I should fight my equals in strength and capacity!'

'You do not have the temperament of a warrior, Karna. Your ego gets in the way of your skills,' replied Bhishma. 'Sit down!'

Karna's eyes blazed with anger. He turned to Duryodhana and said, 'Do not doubt my loyalty, friend, but I will not fight as long as this arrogant old man commands your forces! I will wait for my moment of glory after he has left the battlefield.'

On both sides, warriors spent the night with their weapons, polishing them and cleaning them. In their minds, they went over the magic words they would need that would power the special weapons they had earned from their teachers and from the gods. They meditated and calmed their minds, they concentrated and focused their energies. In their hearts, they knew that even if they survived the war, the world they were fighting to win would have changed irrevocably.

As the sun rose and the great war drums began to beat, the Kauravas and the Pandavas assembled on different sides of Kurukshetra, the battlefield named for their ancestors. The land was flat and had been prepared for this day. It had been watered to settle the dust, stones and rocks had been moved aside so that men, animals and chariots could move swiftly without obstruction.

Horses neighed as they waited and tossed their heads making the bells on their harnesses jingle, elephants blew air noisily through their trunks and shifted restlessly, battle banners fluttered in the morning breeze and the sun glinted on swords and shields and spears and lances and armour.

Suddenly, a great silence descended, as if the universe itself was holding its breath. The breeze died down and the animals were still. The sound of Panchajanya rang through the air and the spell was broken. Horses, elephants, chariots, foot soldiers surged forward and the battle began. Sanjaya began to tell Dhritarashtra all that he could see.

Even without Karna, the first day of fighting went well for the Kauravas. Bhishma, Drona and Kripa were invincible, their skills undiminished by age, and each sent several hundred soldiers to their deaths. Bhishma roared as he brandished his weapons, Drona's hands moved so fast that they were just a blur and Kripa's sword flashed like lightning through the dust that rose from his chariot wheels. Each of them was like a small army in himself and the Pandavas suffered heavy losses.

The next day was the same even though Krishna drove Arjuna's chariot into the thick of battle where he could do the most damage. The Kaurava armies were bigger and better equipped but everyone knew that the real difference between the opposing forces was Grandfather Bhishma. His strategies were unbeatable, his battle formations – the heron, the tortoise, the crocodile, the trident – were impenetrable. Bhishma was taller than most men and it seemed as if he was everywhere. His battle banner with its golden palm tree surrounded by stars fluttered and danced as if with the joy of imminent victory. Duryodhana was pleased with his commanders and each night, after the fighting was done, he complimented them for what they had achieved and thanked them. Karna continued to brood in silence, sitting unarmed and frustrated in his tent as he watched his friends and comrades celebrate their successes.

Day after day, men and animals died by the thousands on Kurukshetra. The ground that had been dry and flat on the first day was now rutted with the marks of chariot wheels and slick with the blood of kings and princes and common soldiers alike. Dust had turned to mud, vultures wheeled in the skies above, jackals howled on the edge of battle and death hung in the air like a dark cloud. All night, the groans of injured and dying men could be heard but there was no way to stop the war.

Yudhishthira called his council together. He said gravely, 'It is

Bhishma that we have to stop. He is our grandfather, we have played in his lap, he has fed us with his own hands and he has tended to our scrapes and bruises when we were children. But if we do not kill him, we will lose this war.'

Arjuna said, 'Grandfather has a boon that he can choose the moment of his own death. We cannot kill him but we can take him out of battle, he will die when he wants to.'

The men were silent, each thinking what it meant to kill the old man who loved them, the great warrior who could not be defeated by any other on earth.

'There is only one thing we can do,' said Yudhishthira. 'We must ask Bhishma how we can kill him. I will go to him now.'

Tears streaming down his cheeks, Yudhishthira went to meet Bhishma. He said, 'Grandfather, you are impossible to kill and you kill hundreds of men each day. We will lose this war if you remain on the battlefield. Tell me, how do we kill you?'

Bhishma looked away and said quietly, 'I will lay down my arms if a woman stands before me on the field of the Kurus. Go now, my son. Do what you must.'

Yudhishthira came back with Bhishma's words ringing in his head. Krishna said, 'There is a young soldier who has been fighting on our side for all these days. His name is Shikhandi. Bhishma will not fight when he is confronted by him. Let Shikhandi fight along with Arjuna tomorrow.'

It was the tenth day of the war. With a heavy heart, Arjuna rode out in his chariot with Shikhandi by his side. Krishna drove straight to where Bhishma was, as tall and unshakeable as a mountain, his weapons slicing and piercing and ripping through those who attacked him. He smiled when he saw Arjuna's chariot approaching.

'Put Shikhandi in front of you, quickly!' shouted Krishna, above the din of battle.

As soon as Bhishma saw Shikhandi, he laid down his weapons. 'I see you, Amba,' he whispered. 'You have returned, as you promised, to be my death. Come, take your revenge!' He turned away and prepared himself for the onslaught of Arjuna's arrows.

But no matter how many arrows pierced his body, mighty Bhishma stood erect and proud. 'How long can I keep shooting at this magnificent

old man?' wondered Arjuna as tears blurred his vision. Finally, Bhishma fell out of his chariot, streams of blood flowing from his wounds. But because his arms and legs and back were full of arrows, his body did not touch the ground.

A great shout went up that Bhishma had fallen. Some say that it was Krishna who shouted out the news. The battle stopped as every soldier honoured the old man whose life had been so exceptional.

The Pandavas and Kauravas gathered around their grandfather. They lifted him carefully and moved him from the battlefield. Bhishma lay on his bed of arrows and asked for a pillow to support his head. Princes ran hither and thither and brought soft pillows of silk and satin, stuffed with soft feathers of white-winged geese. But Bhishma refused them all and looked over at Arjuna. Arjuna picked three unerring arrows from his quiver and shot them into the ground under Bhishma's head. With a fourth arrow he pierced the earth so that a fountain of cool, clear water sprang up near Bhishma's mouth.

Bhishma sighed and laid his head back on the pillow of arrows that suited the final rest of a great warrior. 'Go now, my children,' he said. 'Finish the war that you have started. I will cease to breathe when the sun begins its northern journey across the skies.'

The Sacrifice of the Sons

Ugrashravas said:

Years before, when the Pandavas had been in exile in the forest, they met a brahmin who asked them to help him find the stick with which he lit the sacred fires for the rituals that he had to perform. He said that a deer had taken it from him and he begged the Pandavas to track the deer and retrieve the stick.

The Pandavas searched high and low, they searched together and separately and soon they grew tired and thirsty, for the day was hot and the weather was dry. Nakula climbed a tree and saw a lake in the distance. He told his brothers that he would fetch water for them all while they rested. He was gone for a long time and Sahadeva began to worry. 'I'll check why Nakula still hasn't come back,' he said as he set off in the direction that his brother had taken.

But he did not return either and so Arjuna went in search of the twins. Bhima was impatient, and when there was no sign of Arjuna, he slashed his way through the trees in search of the lake. Finally, Yudhishthira could wait for his brothers no longer and, anxiously, he followed the path that they had taken.

Yudhishthira eventually found the lake that Nakula had seen. He was about to drink from it to quench his blinding thirst when he saw his brothers lying lifeless on the ground. He cried out in alarm but then he knelt at the lake and joined his palms. He said, 'Spirit of the lake, what has happened to my brothers, why do they lie like this on your shores?'

A voice spoke from far away. 'I am the yaksha that guards this lake. You can only drink this water if you answer my questions. Can you do that, Yudhishthira? If not, you will end up like your brothers.'

'I can try,' replied Yudhishthira.

The yaksha asked, 'What has more patience than the earth?'

'A mother bringing up her children.'

'What is swifter than the wind?'

'Thought is swifter than the wind.'

'Who is the traveller's friend?'

'Learning.'

'What is the most precious possession?'

'Knowledge is the most precious of all.'

'What is happiness?'

'Being content is happiness.'

'Who is the enemy?'

'Anger.'

'What is ignorance?'

'Not understanding one's duties and responsibilities.'

The yaksha asked many more questions and Yudhishthira answered them all to his satisfaction. 'This is my final question,' the yaksha said. 'What is the greatest miracle?'

Yudhishthira gazed into the distance and said softly, 'That death is our constant companion and yet we live as if we are immortal!'

'Drink, Yudhishthira, and revive your brothers. I am your father, Dharma, and you have made me happy with your answers. Live by what you have told me and you will prosper!'

Yudhishthira bowed to his father. He touched his brothers' lips with water and they awoke, as if from a dream. They drank together and refreshed themselves and made their way back to where they lived in the forest.

Vaishampayana said:

Duryodhana had been fighting valiantly all along. In the shadow of the Pandavas when they were growing up together, no one had noticed that he, too, was an exceptional fighter. Duryodhana fought fairly and abided by the rules of battle, he appreciated and rewarded his men when they did well and he was also quick to be with them when they were injured. His arrogance, his impatience and bad temper were nowhere in evidence once the war began and the soldiers said to each other, 'Look at Duryodhana, he is so brave, so noble. He does not distinguish between the kings and princes that fight for him and us.'

When Bhishma was felled by Shikhandi and Arjuna, Duryodhana felt that it was time to make Drona the commander of the Kaurava armies. He went to Karna and said, 'My friend, Bhishma is no longer fighting, your time has come. But I would like to ask Drona, our teacher, to lead our forces. After Bhishma, he is our most experienced warrior and has fought many battles against large armies. Besides, I owe him both respect and gratitude. In all these bloody days of death and destruction, all our elders – Bhishma, Drona and Kripa – have fought for us with complete dedication. Whatever they have felt about our enemies, the Pandavas, they have fought for our victory.'

'I will fight under Drona,' said Karna. His eyes lit up, for he was eager to be on the battlefield.

Drona took over the command of the armies and developed his own plans and strategies. He decided it was time to focus on the Pandavas themselves. He knew that Yudhishthira was the weakest of all the brothers on the battlefield and that capturing him would have a huge impact on the soldiers that he led. But he also knew that the Pandavas never left Yudhishthira unprotected and so he would have to make sure that Arjuna was engaged elsewhere when he attacked his brother.

Drona devised a cunning plan – some of the Kaurava allies would attack one flank of the Pandava armies which would draw both Arjuna and Krishna away from the main battle. Then the Kauravas would advance to the centre of the fighting in the dreaded chakravyuha formation. It was in the shape of a disc and seven concentric circles of warriors rotated inside it as it moved forward. Only Arjuna and Krishna knew the secret of how to enter and exit this formation and kill the warriors who were always moving. In their absence, the chakravyuha could be used to its full destructive power.

Arjuna and Krishna heard about the surprise attack but before they left to take care of it, Arjuna said to his most beloved son, born from Krishna's sister, Subhadra, 'Abhimanyu, you have proved yourself in battle, even though you are only sixteen years old. I leave you to guard Yudhishthira, our king. Do not leave him alone, fight beside him at all times!'

'I will, father,' said Abhimanyu and vanished in a cloud of dust as he made his way towards his uncle.

Before long, a cry went up around Kurukshetra. 'Chakravyuha! Chakravyuha!' Soldiers yelled in fear and confusion and began to scatter as the terrifying disc formation ploughed forward, heading towards Yudhishthira and Abhimanyu. Yudhishthira wheeled his chariot around and shouted for Bhima. 'Send for Arjuna! He is the only one who knows how to break this disc and come out alive!'

Bhima shouted back, 'He has gone to protect our western flank with Krishna. We have to deal with the disc on our own!'

Abhimanyu spoke up. 'Uncle, I can do this, I can penetrate the chakravyuha. When my mother was pregnant with me, I heard my father explain this to her – how to get in and how to inflict the maximum damage. He drew a diagram of it on the seashore and showed her where to enter.'

Yudhishthira clapped the boy, his young face bright in the sunlight, on the shoulder and said, 'You are truly your father's son. You will save us today!'

'But there is one thing,' said Abhimanyu. 'I know how to go in but I do not know how to get out. My mother fell asleep before my father finished explaining and the waves of the sea washed away the picture he had made.'

'Never fear,' interrupted Bhima. 'Just get in there, we will be right behind you. Me, your other uncles and all our best warriors will follow you into the disc and we will force a way out.'

Abhimanyu gathered his weapons, his sword and shield, his spears and his arrows and his bow, Raudra, which had been given to him by Krishna. Amidst the tumult of the men and horses and chariots around him, he stood in silence for a moment as he collected his thoughts and focused his energy. He brought his mind to a single point of concentration as his father had taught him. Then, with a great shout, he sped towards the disc.

Abhimanyu was without fear – he used every weapon he had and he kept his mind on the manoeuvres that would let him enter the deadly formation. Knowing that his uncles were behind him, he penetrated the first circle of warriors without any trouble at all. He heard the clash of swords, the shouts of victory and the cries of pain.

Abhimanyu attacked the second circle, his arms whirling as he brought down men in every direction. Deeper and deeper he went, into the heart of the disc, not noticing that the shouts and cries behind him had ceased. Suddenly, he found himself in a clear space, alone. 'Uncles!' he shouted. 'Where are you? I have reached the centre of the chakravyuha! Come and help me get past this final obstacle!'

Slowly, the empty space at the heart of the disc began to close inwards. Abhimanyu saw Drona, Kripa, Kritavarma, Duryodhana, Karna, Jayadratha, Ashwatthama, Shalya, even Dushasana, circling him, their footsteps steady, their weapons drawn. He saw their sons and their cousins, each one with a single focus – himself.

Abhimanyu leapt and spun and slashed and cut and ripped and stabbed, his arrows flew, his sword glinted, his spears whistled through the air as he killed and wounded many. But the collective might of the experienced Kaurava warriors was too much for the young fighter when they attacked him together.

Karna broke his bow, Kripa killed his chariot driver, Kritavarma slew his horses, Drona and Ashwatthama destroyed his sword and shield. Abhimanyu picked up a chariot wheel but Kripa cut it in half.

Abhimanyu had no weapons left. The Kaurava warriors closed in on him and together they raised their arms and stabbed him. Blood covered the ground and Abhimanyu died, killed by his family's enemies and by men who loved his father.

Arjuna returned to the Pandava camp late that night, flushed with victory. He was greeted by a terrible silence. He said, 'What is this? Why is there no rejoicing? Why does Abhimanyu not greet me with news of the war?'

Yudhishthira said, 'The Kauravas used the chakravyuha against us and Abhimanyu went in.'

Arjuna held up his hand. 'You let my sixteen-year-old son enter the disc alone?' he asked in disbelief.

Bhima said, 'We followed him, Arjuna, but Jayadratha blocked us and we were cut off.'

'Where is my son?' whispered Arjuna.

Draupadi came forward, her face streaked with tears. 'Come,' she said and led Arjuna by the hand to where Abhimanyu's body lay.

Across the battlefield of Kurukshetra, the Kaurava camp also wept for Abhimanyu. 'We killed a child today,' Drona said, sadly.

The next morning, Arjuna swore that he would kill Jayadratha before the sun set. 'If I do not kill him before the day ends, I will kill myself by stepping into a fire,' he said as he applied a streak of sacred ash across his forehead. Krishna tried to stop him from taking this terrible oath but Arjuna's grief at the death of his son was as deep as the ocean and he was not going to change his mind.

Drona knew that Arjuna had sworn to kill Jayadratha that day and so he did all that he could to protect his ally, who was also the husband of Duryodhana's sister. He used small but complex formations of warriors, one after the other, to keep Arjuna away from Jayadratha. The battle continued with no victor and the shadows grew long as the sun moved further and further into the western skies. Arjuna was getting frustrated at not being able to get close enough to the man he wanted to kill.

Krishna had to do something to save Arjuna from the vow he had made to take the war to its rightful conclusion. Quietly, he reached for Sudarshana, his discus, and flung it towards the sun. Darkness descended slowly and the Kaurava warriors who had been protecting

Jayadratha began to withdraw – there was no fighting after sunset, they knew. Jayadratha stepped out from behind Duryodhana and laughed out loud, mocking Arjuna and his promise.

Krishna said, 'Quick, Arjuna, use the Pashupata and cut off Jayadratha's head!'

As Arjuna released the deadly weapon, the sun came out again from behind the shadow of Sudarshana. Krishna had created a false sunset, the day of fighting was not over. Jayadratha was killed by the weapon that Shiva had given Arjuna long ago in the icy mountains.

It was now the fourteenth day of the war. Countless men had been slain, some say millions had lost their lives fighting on one side or the other. Drona commanded his forces expertly and inflicted losses upon the enemy but it was Karna who held each day for the Kauravas, killing mighty warriors as well as thousands of soldiers with his magical weapons and his skill. He and Arjuna had met on the battlefield a few times and each time they had withdrawn from each other, as if holding back for a more decisive encounter. But the Pandavas were getting worried about Karna – they could not sustain the losses that he inflicted on their men every day.

Krishna said to Bhima, 'Call your son, Ghatotkacha. He promised to come when you need him. This is the moment, he will strike fear in the hearts of the Kauravas with his huge size and his fearsome appearance.'

In a flash, Ghatotkacha was at his father's side. Bhima embraced his giant son, he kissed his hairy cheeks and stroked his massive arms. 'I have missed you,' he said gently. The young rakshasa picked up his burly father and twirled him around as if he was as light as a feather.

Ghatotkacha joined the battle with abandon. He crushed soldiers under his enormous feet, he squeezed the life out of them with his huge hands, he stuffed them into his mouth that was as large as a mountain cave. No weapons had any effect on him, he swatted arrows and spears off his body as if they were flies, laughing as he did so. And besides, his powers of illusion made him hard to see. He used his magic powers to create walls of fire, rivers of mud and clouds of stinging insects. He fought without stopping and without fatigue, tormenting the enemy warriors and causing thousands upon thousands of deaths.

Duryodhana was very agitated. 'Do something, Karna! You are the only one who can stop this monster. Use your special weapons against him, come on!'

Karna's heart sank. 'I am keeping them for Arjuna,' he said.

'You will kill Arjuna with your fighting skills, not your special weapons,' shouted Duryodhana. 'Do not delay, Karna, we don't have the luxury of time!'

Karna did all he could but nothing would stop the giant. Finally, he pulled out the magnificent unerring spear that could be used only once – Indra had given it to him in exchange for the golden armour that he was born with. He looked over at Duryodhana who yelled, 'Use it, Karna!'

The spear flew from Karna's hand and pierced Ghatotkacha's chest. The rakshasa boy fell to the ground, lifeless, and thousands of soldiers were crushed under his massive body. The Kauravas cheered but Karna knew that he had lost his most potent weapon against Arjuna.

Hidimbi rushed to the battlefield when she heard about the death of her son. She and Bhima cradled his body and wept, each whispering endearments to their beloved child in their own language. In the distance, Krishna danced, alone, smiling, because he knew that Arjuna's life had been saved.

By now, all the rules of battle had been put aside and fighting continued through the night. Like Bhishma, Drona, too, was invincible. There was nothing he could not do on the battlefield, no warrior that he could not overcome. He had killed Virata, who had sheltered the Pandavas in their last year of exile, and Drupada, his old enemy. Even though Drupada's son, Dhrishtadyumna, had been born to kill his father's rival, Drona gave him a spirited fight and forced the younger man to withdraw.

The Pandavas knew that the time had come for them to kill another one of their teachers. 'But how do we kill him?' asked Bhima. 'All that he taught us, he knows better.'

Krishna said, 'Drona will put down his weapons when a man of honour speaks a lie.'

Bhima said, 'I know that he'll stop fighting if he thinks his son has been killed. Ashwatthama is a great warrior and he is not easy to defeat, but I have a plan.' He rushed off, and a few minutes later, the Pandavas heard a great commotion. Elephants trumpeted, Bhima roared, there was a thud and a crash and then Bhima appeared before his brothers, panting. 'I have done it, I have killed Ashwatthama!' He paused and caught his breath. 'I named an elephant Ashwatthama and killed it. Ashwatthama is dead!'

Word spread like wildfire and both camps were buzzing with the news of the death of Ashwatthama. Drona heard it, too, and he stopped in his tracks. He pulled away from the battlefield and asked, 'Is this true? Is my son dead?' He sent for Yudhishthira and looked him straight in the eye. 'You tell me, is my son dead?'

Yudhishthira had never told a lie in his entire life. He looked back at his teacher and said, 'Ashwatthama . . . is dead!' Yudhishthira had whispered 'the elephant' and that very moment Krishna ordered a clamour of bells and drums and pipes.

Drona did not hear the words that would have allowed him to keep fighting. A sob tore through his body and he laid down his weapons. As Drona raised his head, Dhrishtadyumna emerged from the darkness and sliced through his neck with a single arc of his sword. Drona was dead. And Yudhishthira's chariot which until then had never touched the ground settled on the blood-soaked earth.

The Last of the Great Warriors

Ugrashravas said:

After Drona's death, Karna became the commander of the Kaurava armies. The fighting went on. More and more men were killed. The battlefield was littered with broken bodies, splintered chariots and shattered weapons. The animals of death came closer and closer and at night, if there was ever a silence, all that could be heard was the howling of jackals.

Bhima killed Dushasana as he had promised to do when Draupadi was humiliated in public. He ripped open Dushasana's chest and let Draupadi dip her hands in his blood before she tied back her hair that she had worn loose since the day of the gambling match. By pulling back her blood-drenched hair, Draupadi, too, had fulfilled the vow she had made on that day so long ago.

Bhima said, 'I have drunk Dushasana's blood, but this is not over yet, dear wife. I still have to kill Duryodhana and I will smash his thigh before he dies. The end of the war is close now. We will soon have avenged all that was done to you.' Draupadi couldn't smile but she caressed mighty Bhima's arm in thanks.

Duryodhana was devastated by the death of his brother Dushasana. His face wore a blank expression, his eyes were dull and tired, his limbs ached and he was unable to sleep. In the dark night, as the jackals howled and the owls hooted, he sought comfort with his only friend, Karna. But Karna had no hope to offer as he, too, was counting the days that were left of his life. The two warriors sat together in silence, thinking about the choices that they had made and the separate destinies that had brought them to this moment. Duryodhana reflected on the fact that his stubbornness had caused a war that had killed his sons, his brothers and their sons, too. Karna thought about the brothers that he could not claim, one of whom would soon kill him. In their hearts, they both knew that the Age of Kali, the last age of the universe, had begun.

It would be the age of destruction, of hatred and greed, and the earth would groan under the weight of humans and their actions. Water would be scarce and fire would prevail, storm winds would howl across deserts but they would bring no rain, green fields would become barren, bees and butterflies would no longer be seen. Birds would fall silent, the air would turn grey and heavy and, through the thick haze that covered everything, the sun would be pale and seem like the moon.

Karna gazed across Kurukshetra at the flickering lights of the Pandava camp and sighed heavily. Duryodhana turned to him. 'Tomorrow, my friend, you must fight as you have never fought before.'

'There is no other choice,' said Karna. 'Not for me, not for you, not for the men that we lead.' He held out his hand to Duryodhana. 'Come,' he said. 'It will soon be morning and the battles will resume.' Duryodhana embraced Karna and went back to his own tent.

Vaishampayana said:

It was the seventeenth day of the war. As the darkness withdrew from the skies, Karna prepared himself with his morning worship of the sun. He picked out his best arrows and tested the string on his bow, he sharpened his spears and swords and scoured the grip on his shield. Shalya, who was Madri's brother and the uncle of Nakula and Sahadeva, had been tricked by Duryodhana into fighting for the Kauravas. When he realised what had happened, Shalya promised Yudhishthira that he would drive Karna's chariot on the day of his decisive battle with Arjuna and keep him distracted and demoralised.

As Karna was inspecting his chariot, Shalya came to him and said, 'Let me drive for you today. I am an expert charioteer, anyone will tell you that. And I know Krishna's tactics well.' Karna agreed and handed over the reins of the chariot to Shalya.

As they rode out, Shalya said, 'Gandiva is a magnificent bow, and in Arjuna's hands, it is impossible to counter. Have you thought about how you will defeat him?' Karna was silent but his hand went to his own bow, Vijaya, and he stroked it, muttering a prayer. Shalya went on, 'Krishna and Arjuna together are like one warrior. I am sure of my skills, are you sure of yours? What if Arjuna defeats you?'

Karna said, 'When I saw Bhishma and Drona defeated, I understood that there is more to winning a battle than skill. Those great men fell to their fate, not to the weapons that struck them. My fate will decide whether or not I can win this battle. If I am to die in battle, I will make sure that I do not die a coward.'

After a short pause, Karna spoke again. 'Shalya, I know your loyalty lies with your nephews on the Pandava side. You speak like this to discourage me. But neither I nor you have any control over what will happen today. Let me fight at my best.' Shalya felt shame at Karna's words, for he realised that he was in the presence of a truly exceptional man.

The soldiers stood at the edges of Kurukshetra, knowing that this battle would decide the outcome of the war. If Arjuna defeated Karna, victory would belong to the Pandavas, and if Karna won, Duryodhana would be the undisputed king of the Kaurava lands. Even the gods gathered in the skies above the battlefield to watch these two great warriors, equally matched in skill and in divine weapons, fight to the end. Each pulled the string of his bow and their chariot drivers snapped their reins, urging their horses forward.

Arjuna and Karna were as strong and mighty as two great tuskers in a forest. They attacked each other ferociously – the air grew thick with a rain of arrows, some had crescent heads, others had forked tips, some turned into vicious snakes, others into boar heads with sharp fangs. No matter how many arrows hit them, the brothers fought on and on. Their swords clashed, their spears collided and cut each other off in mid-flight. Their horses reared and neighed and their chariot wheels scarred the ground as Krishna and Shalya executed complex manoeuvres so that their rider could hold better positions from which to aim at his opponent.

Karna seemed to be gaining the upper hand and Krishna said to Arjuna, 'Come on, Arjuna! Look, the Kauravas behind this son of a charioteer are already celebrating because they think Karna has defeated you. Where is your concentration, where are your divine weapons, this is not the time to hesitate!'

Arjuna summoned up his mightiest weapons and unleashed them, but Karna was calm as he sent his arrows towards Arjuna. He snapped the string of Gandiva, and each time Arjuna added another string, Karna's arrow pierced that, too. Karna decided that it was time to use his deadly snake weapon. He nocked it into his bow and aimed for Arjuna's head. Shalya said, 'Aim lower, you might miss his head!' But Karna ignored him. He released the weapon and a flash of light emerged from his bow.

In that instant, Krishna saw what had happened and forced his horses to kneel so that Arjuna's chariot sank low to the ground. Karna's mighty weapon grazed the top of Arjuna's crown which fell harmlessly behind him. Arjuna looked at his fallen crown and his focus and concentration returned. Krishna saw the determination in his friend's eyes and knew that Karna had only minutes to live.

Suddenly, Karna's chariot sank into the soft mud, so deep that his horses could not pull it forward. Shalya threw down the reins and fled. Karna knew that he now had to use the only weapon he had left, one that would kill thousands more than only Arjuna, who was its target.

He tried to recall the magic words that would summon the weapon that Parashurama had given him, but his mind was blank. Then he remembered the insect that had bored through his leg and his teacher's angry curse. He realised that the weapon that could have saved him was out of reach.

Karna closed his eyes. He saw death but he roared and jumped out of his unbalanced chariot. He bent over the stuck wheel and tried to lift it out of the mud. Arjuna sent a shower of arrows in his direction. Karna shouted, 'Arjuna! You are a kshatriya! You cannot attack me when I am unarmed and helpless. Do not break the warrior's code of conduct! Wait and I will fight you in a minute.'

Krishna yelled back, 'You speak of honour, you speak of a code of conduct! Where was honour when you watched Draupadi being disrobed in public? Where was your warrior's code when the six of you attacked Abhimanyu together? Your life is over Karna, all your misdeeds have come back to haunt you!'

Arjuna stood as if paralysed, staring at the glorious man who stood helpless in the mud before him. Krishna said, 'Now, Arjuna, this is the moment. Kill him!' Arjuna lifted Gandiva and picked an unerring arrow. He released the arrow and it pierced Karna's chest. A great light shot out of the fallen warrior's body and flew into the sky as the sun went behind a cloud. Karna's eyes were open as he drew his last breath and they were fixed on Arjuna.

Krishna drove Arjuna back to the Pandava camp to bathe and dress his wounds. Arjuna could not understand why he was so extraordinarily tired and why his heart was so heavy – he had just defeated his most feared opponent and the victory of the Pandavas was now certain. After days of fighting, his limbs were weary and his arms ached from the thousands of arrows he had shot over the seventeen days. He wanted to lie down and sleep, but he knew that his brothers still counted on him to lead them. He was quiet as the celebrations around him grew louder and louder.

Duryodhana retreated from the clamour of the camp to be alone so that he could mourn the man who had meant more to him than any of his brothers. He also knew that Karna's death announced the defeat of the Kauravas and he thought again about all that he had done and not done to bring the conflict with his cousins to this terrible end. He decided to talk to Bhishma, the grandfather who had watched it all unfold, even before Duryodhana and his brothers and cousins had been born.

He went to where the old man lay on his bed of arrows, still glorious and commanding. He knelt beside him and said, 'It is I, Duryodhana. I have never been your favourite, but now I have come to you, grandfather. Help me understand all that has happened. I have lost my best friend and I cannot live another day without him. The others can finish the war without me, I am no use to anyone any more.'

Bhishma reached out and touched Duryodhana's face that was wet with tears. He said, 'Don't grieve for Karna. He died the way he should have, as a great warrior on the battlefield. He was a kshatriya, you know.'

Duryodhana sighed. 'I knew this all along. I tried to save him from the insults that people hurled at him. But I could never prove that he was not a charioteer's son. Who was he, grandfather, you can tell me now.'

'It will break your heart if I tell you, but you must know who he was. You must keep his secret though, for he knew and he didn't tell you or anyone else.'

'Tell me,' said Duryodhana, looking up at the old man.

'He was Kunti's eldest son,' said Bhishma gently.

'He knew this and he still fought his brothers for me!' Duryodhana could not keep his voice down. He wept openly now, deep sobs wracking his body as Bhishma told him how Karna was born and abandoned, how Kunti had gone to see him before the war began to tell him who he was and had begged him to fight alongside the Pandavas and how he had refused because of his love for Duryodhana and his loyalty to the only person who had treated him as an equal. He also told him that Karna knew that he was fated to die fighting Arjuna. Duryodhana kissed Bhishma's hand and stumbled away, determined that he would fight to the end, that he, too, would die honourably for the sake of his beloved Karna.

The sun rose on the eighteenth and final day of the war. The warriors, the kings and princes and soldiers who were still alive, arrayed themselves as usual and waited for the conch to signal the start of fighting. Shalya was now the commander of the Kaurava troops and he led his listless, disheartened men into battle for what would be the last time. At the end of the day, very few of them would be left alive.

One by one, the warriors faced off against each other. The Kaurava forces were vastly reduced and they were tired, the men were wounded and their commanders were without hope. But the Pandavas had the light of victory in their eyes and they spared no one. Satyaki, Shikhandi and Dhrishtadyumna were everywhere, both ahead of and behind Arjuna and Bhima. Nakula killed Karna's sons, Bhima and Shalya fought with no holds barred, they used their maces and attacked each other's bodies.

Shalya was unstoppable and the Pandavas realised why he had been chosen to command the last day of battle. Shalya knew that if he killed Yudhishthira, this could still be a victory for the Kauravas. But Yudhishthira was surrounded by his brothers who did everything they could to demolish Shalya's challenge. Eventually, it was Yudhishthira's lance that slew Shalya.

Duryodhana stepped forward to take Shalya's place and he fought like a man possessed, taking on several Pandava warriors at once. Still it was only a matter of time before the Kauravas surrendered. Sahadeva slew Shakuni and then only Duryodhana, Kripa, Ashwatthama and Kritavarma were left.

Duryodhana's armour was in tatters, his weapons were in pieces. His body was burning. He turned away from Kurukshetra and stumbled towards the cool blue lake that he knew lay at some distance from the battlefield. With his mace in hand, he threw himself into the water.

The Bitter End

Ugrashravas said:

Even though the war raged around him, Bhishma had lain calmly on his bed of arrows. Sometimes, his nephews would come and talk to him, at other times he would be visited by people from his dreams or people from the future and he treated them all equally. He had made up his mind to stay alive until Yudhishthira was crowned king of Hastinapura, because he knew that the war would end with the defeat of the Kauravas. He also knew that had things been different, he would have been Yudhishthira's guide and counsellor when he was king. He wanted to share all that he had learned about kingship with

Yudhishthira who, he was sure, would not make the mistakes that his uncle Dhritarashtra had.

Bhishma recognised that Yudhishthira was a man of thought rather than a man of action. He was honourable and fair and would decide what needed to be done after discussion and, then, solitary contemplation. Yudhishthira was also the son of Dharma, the god of righteousness, and he was born to be king. Bhishma had no doubt that Yudhishthira had learned much from his own behaviour at the gambling match and from his conversations with wise men during the exile in the forest. Even the war had taught him many things about how to be a good king.

When the last of the great warriors had died, Yudhishthira came often to sit with Grandfather Bhishma. Sometimes he asked questions and sometimes the old man who had seen so much just talked. 'My son, the most important thing that a king has to learn is that he is alone. He cannot share his thoughts and, often, people will not tell him what he needs to hear because they fear his displeasure. And yet, he must choose men that he can trust to give him advice and who know more than he does about certain things – the army, the treasury, crops and animals, spies and informers. These men will help him look after his people for it is the king's first duty to keep his citizens prosperous and happy. A king must protect the weak and control the strong. Justice lies with him as does mercy.'

On another occasion, Bhishma spoke to Yudhishthira about the four ages because knowing how the world changes over time would help him be a better ruler. 'Long ago, there was a perfect world. People were good to each other, there was no sickness and disease, the earth gave of her bounty to all and everyone was happy with what they received. Virtue and righteousness were everywhere and dharma was strong. But then, things began to change, so slowly that no one noticed. Even dharma gets worn down and used up, and as the ages passed from the first to the second to the third, human beings grew interested in power and wealth for themselves, they pressed the earth for more than she could provide and they began to fight over things they thought they needed. Anger and greed and hatred entered the lives of men and women, they grew further and further from their neighbours in mind and heart.

'When this war is over, Yudhishthira, the world will enter the fourth and last age. There will be sickness and there will be death, there will be cruelty and violence, everything that we thought would last forever will perish. You will have to rule in this, the worst of all ages, when dharma is under attack from all sides.

'Truth will not be distinguished from falsehood, the bad will appear as the good and people will have lost the ability to use their reason. In the time that I have left on earth, before my chosen day of death, listen to me and I will tell you all that I know. It is not your successes that make you who you are, it is your failures. I have learned from my mistakes. You will also make mistakes, my son, but they will be your own mistakes and not those of your forefathers.'

And so they spoke for days and nights together, Devavrata Gangadatta who became known as Bhishma when he renounced kingship for his father's sake and Yudhishthira Dharmaraja who had fought a war with his cousins for the throne of his ancestors, a war that ushered in the end of Time itself.

Vaishampayana said:

Bhima was not done with his revenge yet. For him, the war would not be over until he had smashed Duryodhana's thigh and killed him. At the end of the eighteenth day of fighting, along with his brothers and Krishna, he went in search of Duryodhana. They had heard that Duryodhana was lying under the water of the lake, holding his breath. Yudhishthira approached the shore of the lake and shouted, 'Duryodhana, come out and fight! Don't be a coward, come out and face the consequences of your actions!'

Duryodhana roared back, still under water. 'I'm resting. Why are you disturbing me with your meaningless chatter? Go, prepare yourselves, I'll be back to fight very soon!' After a short pause, he spoke again. 'Take this kingdom, Yudhishthira, this is what you wanted. I have no interest in it now, the people that I loved and would have shared it with are dead. You take it – this blood-soaked earth, this country of widows and orphans, this land of men with broken limbs and vacant eyes.'

'You are defeated, Duryodhana,' Yudhishthira replied. 'This

kingdom is no longer yours to give away! Accept the truth of your situation and come out of the water.'

'I had something you will never have, Yudhishthira. I had the love of my people – I was a good king, I was just, I was fair, I was happy. I laughed, I danced, I loved my wives, I was good to my friends. I am ready to leave this earthly life.'

'Then stand up and fight!' shouted Bhima. 'I will take you on. Pick your weapon.'

Duryodhana rose from the water. He stood tall and proud – his body was firm even though some of his wounds were bleeding, his muscles were taut, his legs were strong and his arms were mighty. 'For you, Bhima, I pick the mace. Balarama has taught us both – let's see which of us was the better student!'

Balarama happened to be returning from a pilgrimage and was quickly brought to witness the duel between his students. The fighters honoured their teacher who reminded them of the rules that they had to obey as they fought, the most important of which was that an opponent could not be struck below the waist. Sanjaya, who had described the entire war to Dhritarashtra, watched from a distance.

Duryodhana struck first, it was a mighty blow and Bhima reeled backwards. He quickly recovered his balance and threw himself into the confrontation. It was a brutal form of combat, blow after blow that thudded into the body. But the two were evenly matched – what Duryodhana had in skill, Bhima had in strength. They heaved and thrust, they groaned and roared and the earth shook under their feet as they held nothing back. But soon, it was clear that Duryodhana, lighter on his feet and with sharper skills, had the upper hand. Bhima was tiring. He had started to stagger and his aim was no longer as accurate.

A heavy blow from Duryodhana brought Bhima to his knees and it seemed as if he would not be able to stand up again. He leaned on his mace and looked despairingly at Krishna. Krishna shone with a mysterious light and it seemed as if he was smiling. Slowly and deliberately, he slapped his thigh and nodded at Bhima. Bhima heaved himself up and lumbered towards Duryodhana. He swung his mace. Duryodhana was not expecting a low blow and did not protect himself as Bhima's weapon smashed into his thighs. He screamed in agony and collapsed to the ground.

Panting and sweating, Bhima went over to Duryodhana and began to kick the fallen warrior. 'My final promise has been kept, Duryodhana! That thigh you patted when you humiliated our wife has been shattered. Your life is over. Go to hell!'

At once, Yudhishthira was at his side and said, 'Stop it, Bhima. Duryodhana is a king, he is worthy of honour. You cannot behave like this. Besides, he is our cousin, we have grown up together. This is not how we celebrate.'

Balarama was so angry with Bhima's ignoble blow and with his behaviour after his victory that he left without saying a word to his student.

Duryodhana raised himself as much as he could and said, 'You cheated, Bhima, you will know that till your dying day. You were losing and you hit me below the waist – you could not have defeated me if you had fought fairly.' He grimaced with pain as he turned himself to face Krishna. 'And you, you have broken every rule that you made us swear to! I saw you slap your thigh, I saw the signal you gave Bhima.

His victory over me is a lie. But I am dying with honour, I couldn't care less about the world you live in after me.' He groaned. 'Leave me, all of you. Let my last sight not be of the family that has always hated me and their friend who has brought me to this.' Duryodhana closed his eyes and the Pandavas and Krishna moved away.

Krishna said that he would go to Gandhari and Dhritarashtra and tell them what had happened. He advised the Pandavas not to come with him because he was sure that, despite her grief, Gandhari's anger would be fierce and dangerous. When Krishna got to the palace, he realised that Sanjaya had already told the old king and queen about the death of their eldest and most beloved son. Krishna held Gandhari in his arms as she wept for all her sons and her grandsons who had been killed. But she wept most of all for the unfair killing of her firstborn son, Duryodhana, the king, and she blamed Krishna for doing nothing to prevent the terrible war that had left her childless.

The duel between Bhima and Duryodhana had also had other witnesses, hidden and silent: Ashwatthama, still seething with rage over the killing of his father, Drona, Kripa, who had taught both the Pandavas and the Kauravas when they were young princes, and Kritavarma, who had led the Yadava forces within the Kaurava army. Ashwatthama had already sworn revenge against the Pandavas for the deceitful way in which they had made his father lay down his arms and now Kripa and Kritavarma were repulsed at the way in which Duryodhana had been killed by Bhima.

Ashwatthama bent down beside Duryodhana and took his hand. 'Do not worry, sire, I will make sure the Pandavas regret every single life they have taken. You can enter the next world knowing that your enemies will pay heavily for all that they have done to us!' Duryodhana smiled painfully. Ashwatthama spoke. 'But you must anoint me commander of your forces, I need the authority to attack the Pandavas.'

Duryodhana raised his hand and blessed the young man who knelt before him. Kripa fetched water from the lake and, as he poured it over Ashwatthama's head, he recited the verses that would make him commander of the Kaurava forces which now consisted of only two other men.

Ashwatthama and his companions faded into the gathering dusk and hid in the forest close to the lake. Although his companions quickly fell into exhausted sleep, Ashwatthama stayed awake, plotting the destruction of the Pandavas. His mind flitted from idea to idea. But he had no men to command and the Pandava forces were still strong, despite their losses.

He was staring into the darkness as he thought over his options when, from the corner of his eye, he caught a swift movement. He turned and saw an owl, gliding soundlessly through the night to land in the branches of a tree. The owl was as still as a statue, only its round yellow eyes were visible. Suddenly, the owl rose and attacked a nest in which birds were asleep with their fledglings. Flesh and feathers flew in all directions as the birds chirped in terror and flapped their wings, but the owl made a meal of the young ones and flew away holding the last of them in his claws.

Ashwatthama was transfixed – he had the solution to his problem.

He would attack the Pandava camp at night, when everyone was asleep. His approach would be stealthy and soundless, like the owl's, and he would care nothing for the children that lay asleep in the camp. In a frenzy of excitement, he woke his companions and told them what he had seen and how he had turned that into an idea for their final assault on their enemies.

Kripa and Kritavarma were reluctant to go through with Ashwatthama's plan. They argued that it was against the rules of war but Ashwatthama laughed and said, 'This entire war has been fought by rules that were made to be broken, by deceit and by duplicity!' He mounted his chariot, whipped his horses and rode off towards Kurukshetra. The older men realised that it was better to be with Ashwatthama at this time and they followed him quickly.

When Ashwatthama got to the gate of the camp, an enormous creature blocked his way. The creature was truly hideous with arms and eyes in every direction. It was clad in the bloody skins of dead animals and flames poured from its mouth. Ashwatthama was focused on his own plans and so he was not perturbed by this obstacle. He sent forth his arrows and the creature absorbed them all. Ashwatthama attacked with more of his deadly weapons but, again, to no avail. More irritated at being delayed than frightened, the young warrior tried a few more times to vanquish the creature who was spewing flames and smoke and using all its arms to attack.

Finally, Ashwatthama decided it was time to appease Shiva, by whose grace he had been born. Drona had begged the great god for a son and Shiva had given him Ashwatthama, born with a gem in his forehead that kept him free from hunger, thirst and fatigue. Ashwatthama threw himself forward and prayed. He asked Shiva to appear before him and bless him, to make his enterprise successful, to give him the weapons and the strength to destroy the men who had betrayed his father and who had made a mockery of all that he had taught them.

In a blinding flash of light, Shiva appeared. He was beautiful – the crescent moon shone in his hair, a gleaming snake was coiled around his neck, an orange-gold tiger skin covered the lower part of his body and he held his trident in his right hand. He smiled and said, 'Your time has come, child!' and handed Ashwatthama his own sword. 'This will be all you need.'

Ashwatthama kissed the sword and touched it to his forehead. When he looked up again, the gate to the Pandava camp was open and Shiva and the monstrous creature had both vanished. Ashwatthama saw that Kripa and Kritavarma had caught up with him and he told them to stay at the gate and let no one escape.

Ashwatthama crept into the camp, as dark and as silent as a shadow. First, he sought out Dhrishtadyumna, who had killed his father. He woke him up and made sure that he knew who his killer was. He fell upon Draupadi's brother, kicking and punching him viciously, even though Dhrishtadyumna begged for mercy. He left the prince of Panchala a crumpled heap on the ground. Then he went after Shikhandi and cut his throat with Shiva's sword as he slept.

All around him, Ashwatthama saw the young Pandava princes, the sons and nephews of his father's beloved students. Like Death himself, he sliced the boys to pieces without them even realising that they would never wake up again. He stalked the camp, slashing his divine sword this way and that, never missing a sleeping body.

Kripa and Kritavarma had started a fire at the gate that blazed through the enclosure. Common soldiers were burnt alive as was anybody who tried to leave the camp.

Finally, Ashwatthama's rage subsided and, along with Kripa and Kritavarma, he rushed back to the dying Duryodhana. Ashwatthama knelt before his king and said, 'There is not a living soul in that camp. Our revenge is complete. The Pandavas have been decimated. Go, my lord, go in peace to the world of heroes!' Duryodhana's cracked lips parted and he drew his last breath.

Krishna had known that the Pandava brothers would be in danger from what was left of the Kaurava forces and so he had taken them away for the night to a place of safety. In the morning, they were given the horrific news of the night massacre. Unable to speak, they were led to the camp and shown the slashed bodies of their sons – all of Draupadi's sons were slain as were the sons of all the other wives of the five Pandavas. An entire generation of Pandava princes had been wiped out. Draupadi broke down and wept. She wept for her sons and for all the others boys who had been struck down in a conflict of their fathers' making. She turned to her husbands and said, 'Bring me the jewel from Ashwatthama's forehead. Then I will know that you have killed that savage beast who has done this to my family.'

Krishna and the Pandava brothers went in search of Ashwatthama. Krishna warned them that Ashwatthama still had the deadliest of all weapons, the brahmashiras, in his possession. They found Ashwatthama on the riverbank, praying and meditating along with the sage Vyasa.

Ashwatthama saw them coming towards him and he knew that they intended to kill him. He picked up a blade of grass and powered it with the secret spell that held the brahmashiras. The grass leapt out of his hand and blazed into the sky. 'This will kill the last of the Pandava sons, wherever they are!' he shouted.

The fiery missile headed for Uttara, Abhimanyu's wife, who was carrying his child, Arjuna's grandson, in her womb. Arjuna sent his own deadly weapon after the brahmashiras.

Vyasa cried, 'Stop this! If these weapons collide, a great darkness will fall upon the earth. For twelve years, nothing will grow, the land will be dead, the rivers will dry up, it will be the end of all life!'

Arjuna looked at Krishna who said, 'Call your weapon back.' Arjuna concentrated his energies and closed his eyes. After what seemed like a long time, his weapon fizzed like a damp firework and fell out of the sky.

Vyasa shouted, 'Ashwatthama!'

But the young man did nothing. 'I don't know how to call it back,' he whispered. 'It will do as I asked and go where it must.'

Krishna chased the brahmashiras with his mind and diverted it from Uttara. It landed harmlessly and buried itself in the ground. Ashwatthama hung his head in shame, all anger and desire for revenge drained from his body. Krishna cut the jewel from his forehead and gave it to Yudhishthira.

'Get out, Ashwatthama, you have lost the right to live among humans,' said Krishna. 'And I curse you: you will live forever and your wound will bleed and ooze and cause you unimaginable pain. You will be despised by all and you will suffer until the end of time, because you cannot die!' Ashwatthama slunk away into the forest.

Krishna and the Pandavas went to meet the family elders to tell them about the massacre. They comforted Kunti as she mourned the death of her children's children and then Yudhishthira insisted that they should all ask Gandhari to forgive them for killing her sons. Dhritarashtra turned away from his nephews when he was told they had come to see him but Gandhari agreed to meet them.

Yudhishthira was the first to approach her, and as he bent to touch her feet, Gandhari lifted the edge of the blindfold she had worn since the day she was married. Her gaze fell on Yudhishthira's toe which was instantly charred.

One by one, Gandhari forgave her husband's nephews and she let them all touch her feet, even Krishna. Then in a voice that shook with anger, she said, 'You, Krishna, you have done this! This empty palace, my children lying broken on the battlefield where wild animals sniff their bodies, this is your fault. You could have stopped the war! You had the power, you always knew what was going to happen, you knew that it would end with us standing here among widows and orphans. I curse you, Krishna! Your family, too, will fall upon each other and destroy themselves as ours has done. You, too, will have no living relatives when they are done with one another. And you, you will die alone, unrecognised, you will die like an animal, Krishna!'

Krishna smiled and said, 'I accept your curse, mother. I, too, am your son.'

Aftermath

Vaishampayana said:

After Duryodhana's death and the night massacre, the women, who had stayed in the cities during the war, went to the battlefield to look for their men – their fathers, brothers, sons, grandsons, nephews, uncles, grandfathers, brothers-in-law. Each one of them prayed in her heart that her man would not be found wounded in the back, for that would mean that he had been killed as he was running away. They searched for their heroes in the day under the burning sun and through the night with the light of torches.

The air was filled with the sound of women weeping – they sobbed as they stumbled over bodies they recognised, or wailed because they could not find what was left of their men. They knelt in the mud and bloody gore, their tears falling like rain upon dead faces and broken bodies. Every now and then, a cry of joy would pierce the sadness when a woman found a husband or a brother who was still alive. The wounded were carried back to the city with light steps but the weight of the dead was heavy. Soon, the battlefield turned into a cremation ground as it was often easier to perform the last rites where the bodies lay. For some, there were no sons left to perform these rites and so the sons of other men stepped in to ensure the soul's safe journey to the next world.

Kurukshetra had turned from a field of glory into a field of the dead and dying. Yudhishthira took the Pandavas there to see what their victory had cost. He wanted them to realise that the kingdom they had coveted so much had brought death and destruction to hundreds and thousands of people, including their own subjects. Grimly, the brothers walked through the slush, taking in what they had unleashed, and their hearts grew heavy. Suddenly, Yudhishthira said, 'Wait! Isn't that our mother over there?'

Puzzled at Kunti's presence among those searching for their dead on the battlefield, her sons went quickly to her side and saw that she was weeping over the body of a fallen warrior.

Arjuna was the first to speak. 'Mother, that is Karna. Why do you weep for the death of our mortal enemy? He had sworn to kill me!'

Kunti looked up at her sons, but when she spoke through her tears, it was Yudhishthira that she addressed. 'Karna is your brother, my firstborn son!'

Arjuna and Bhima were speechless but Yudhishthira knelt beside his mother and held her in his arms. 'Did he know?' he asked quietly.

Kunti nodded. 'I told him before the war began because I wanted him to fight on your side, on the side of his brothers. But he chose to be loyal to Duryodhana who had treated him with respect.'

'Why did he not grow up with us, if he was your son?' asked Bhima, who liked to have things explained clearly.

Kunti told her sons how Karna had been born and how she had left him by the riverbank with a prayer that he would be brought up and loved by good people. Arjuna turned away, unable to come to terms with what he had done, but Yudhishthira caressed his older brother's face and wept. 'If I had known you were my brother, I would have surrendered even before fighting. I would have given you the kingdom. This war would never have been fought, these thousands of lives would not have been lost!' He told his brothers that they should perform Karna's funeral rites along with those of the other members of the family, their sons and grandsons and Draupadi's brother, who had been killed.

Inevitably, the moment of Bhishma's passing arrived and, on the day that the sun began its journey to the north, Bhishma died quietly on his bed of arrows, surrounded by the members of his family and watched by heavenly beings. Humans and gods both knew that another like Bhishma would not be born on earth again. After his death, Sanjaya and Vidura persuaded the grieving elders, Kunti, Gandhari and

Dhritarashtra, to leave the city which now held only memories and to live quietly together in the forest.

Yudhishthira took the throne of his ancestors reluctantly and there was little to make him happy. Krishna returned to his own city, Dwarka, Arjuna withdrew into himself, Bhima ate and drank too much, the twins lived their own lives and Draupadi's eyes were haunted by death all the time. But even as some people die, others are born and soon there was some joy in the palace with the birth of Arjuna's grandson. Uttara, Abhimanyu's wife, gave birth to the child that Krishna had saved by diverting Ashwatthama's weapon away from her. The boy was named Parikshit and it was through him that the lineage of the Kaurava heroes would be restored.

Even though Yudhishthira performed all the tasks and rituals and grand sacrifices that were expected of him as a monarch, the kingdom of the Kurus never regained its former glory. There were omens of destruction everywhere – jackals howled, meteors streaked across the sky and were visible even during the day, clouds produced bloody rain. Time was moving forward and the world was preparing for the birth of the last age, the age of despair. After some years, the Pandavas learned that their elders had died in a fire that had swept through the forest in which they had been living their simple lives.

Krishna ruled Dwarka with his brother Balarama but he carried within himself the weight of Gandhari's curse – that his people would kill each other and that his time in the world of humans would soon end.

One day, three great sages came to Dwarka and the young princes of the city decided to play a prank on them. They dressed Krishna's grandson as a woman and said to the sages, 'Sires, this woman is pregnant. Will she give birth to a boy or a girl?'

The sages were not amused and said, 'An iron club will emerge from her body and will destroy your clan!'

That very night, a club was pulled out of the boy's body. Balarama ordered the club to be crushed into a fine powder and scattered in the sea that licked at the shores of his city. But the waves washed the powder back to land and from it grew a thicket of reeds that shone like metal in the sunlight.

Some years later, the Yadava clans, which included the Vrishnis and the Andhakas, came together to celebrate a grand religious festival. When they finished the sacred rituals, they began to drink and grew boisterous and aggressive. Satyaki, who had never forgiven Kritavarma for fighting on Duryodhana's side, became angry. He started to curse Kritavarma and soon they were fighting. Satyaki sliced off Kritavarma's head with his sword.

The Vrishnis and the Andhakas followed the men who had led them into battle and fell upon each other, hitting one another with anything they could find. One by one, they reached for the shining reeds that had grown by the seashore. As the reeds were plucked, they turned into iron clubs and the Yadava clans bludgeoned each other to death.

Not a man was left standing.

Krishna and Balarama had watched from a distance, each lost in his own thoughts. Balarama went into a forest and sat down under a tree. He slowed his breath until it was completely stilled and passed out of his life in the world of humans.

Krishna was now alone and he wanted nothing more than to see his beloved Arjuna once more before he left the earth. He closed his eyes and concentrated on his friend, speaking to him in his mind. Far away in Hastinapura, a sleeping Arjuna heard Krishna's call. He awoke with a start and made preparations to go to Dwarka at once.

Krishna knew that Arjuna had heard him and he was at peace. He went into the same forest as Balarama had and settled at the foot of the same tree where his brother had ceased to breathe. He heaved a great sigh and lay down on the forest floor.

Impelled by fate, a hunter named Jara came to the same place. From a distance, he saw what he thought was the ear of a deer. He picked an iron-tipped arrow from his quiver and placed it in his bow. With a practised motion, he released the arrow, knowing that he would strike his target, and ran to where his arrow had landed. He saw that his arrow had pierced Krishna's heel which was perfectly shaped, as soft and tender as a deer's ear. Krishna's blood flowed from his wound into the earth and when Jara lifted his head on to his lap, he saw that Krishna was radiant and that he was smiling.

Arjuna was ill with grief when he learned that his friend had left the world. He took the news back to Hastinapura and the Pandavas mourned the man who had protected them for so many years, who had helped them win the war and had established them securely as rulers of their ancestral kingdom. Once Krishna had left the world, the Pandavas grew less interested in the affairs of the kingdom and the welfare of their people and soon they placed Parikshit on the throne of Hastinapura. Wearing simple clothes and travelling without their courtiers and retainers, they set off to visit places of pilgrimage. After years of wandering, Yudhishthira decided that it was time for them to go to the northernmost mountains, to the abode of the gods.

The journey was long and rough. The ground they walked on was covered with snow, the slope was steep and the icy wind tore through their rough clothes. Their lips and hands and feet turned blue with cold, but still the five Pandavas and their wife walked on. Draupadi slipped and, before any of her husbands could reach her, she fell down the side of the mountain.

Bhima wailed and asked Yudhishthira, 'This sinless woman, she never did anything wrong in her life. Why has she fallen on our last journey?'

'Even though she promised to love us all, she loved Arjuna the most,' replied the eldest Pandava.

As they walked higher and higher, the twins slipped down the mountain, one after the other. Nakula had been vain about his good looks and Sahadeva about his intelligence. Kunti's three sons trudged on, their heads bent against the driving wind and snow. Arjuna was the next to fall.

'Why, brother, why Arjuna?' asked Bhima.

Yudhishthira said, 'He prided himself on his skills as an archer and said that he would kill all his enemies in a day. He failed to do that.'

'And what will happen to me?' asked Bhima, suddenly frightened. 'Will I reach heaven with you?'

'No, my dear Bhima. You ate too much and you boasted about your strength. You, too, will fall.' Yudhishthira did not look back when Bhima slipped away from him.

Yudhishthira walked on, his thoughts fixed only on the next step that he had to take. Out of the mist, a celestial chariot appeared and Indra, the king of the gods, was seated in it. 'Come, Yudhishthira,' he said. 'You are the only one of your brothers and wife who can enter the realm of the immortals in your human body! But you must leave that dog behind.'

Yudhishthira replied, 'This dog has been with me since I started this journey up the mountain. I cannot leave him here. I will not go any further without him, no matter where you take me.' And Yudhishthira stood firmly where he was.

Indra laughed and in a flash the dog vanished. In its place stood a shining god. 'I am Dharma, your father,' he said to Yudhishthira. 'You are the only one who has remained good and true, as a king and as a human being. You have earned everything that lies ahead of you. Come, Yudhishthira, enter the realms of pleasure with me!'

Along with Indra, Yudhishthira walked towards the light that lay ahead and entered the most beautiful and soothing place he had ever seen. 'But where are my brothers and Draupadi?' he asked, bewildered.

'Forget about them, Yudhishthira, this is what you alone have

earned,' said Indra. 'They were part of your life on earth, you have left all that behind. Enjoy the pleasures before you!'

Yudhishthira looked around and to his great astonishment he saw Duryodhana before him, seated on a throne and blazing with light. He turned away, trembling. 'What is this man doing here? He shamed my wife, he is the reason we fought that bloody war . . .'

'Duryodhana died a hero,' said Indra. 'He deserves to be here.'

'I don't want to be in a place that honours people like him. Take me to my brothers and my wife,' said Yudhishthira quietly.

Indra led Yudhishthira down a path that was difficult to walk on. It was harsh and littered with stones and there was a terrible stench in the air, so bad that Yudhishthira could hardly breathe. It was dimly lit by fires and shadows formed themselves into terrifying shapes. They seemed to be reaching out towards Yudhishthira, trying to entangle him in their arms. Everywhere there were the sounds of sighing and wailing, moans of pain and voices calling out. 'Take me away from here, I cannot bear to hear others suffer like this,' begged Yudhishthira.

Out of the darkness came a cry. 'Yudhishthira, don't leave us, stay here!' Yudhishthira spun around, trying to see where the voice came from and who was calling out to him.

'Stay, Yudhishthira, stay,' called another voice. 'It is not so bad when you are here, we feel a cool breeze, we can smell a gentle fragrance, our pain lessens . . .'

'Who is this, who calls to me?' shouted Yudhishthira.

'It is I, Draupadi.'

'I am Karna!'

'It is Bhima!'

'I am Arjuna!'

'We are Nakula and Sahadeva!' came the voices.

Yudhishthira turned to Indra and said, 'Leave me here. I want to be with my family,' and he sat down on the rocky ground.

Time passed. Yudhishthira began to feel faint with the smell and the heat. He closed his eyes and tried to recall the beloved faces of his brothers and his wife. Suddenly, there was a flash of light. Indra stood before him and the terrible place that he had been in disappeared. 'This was your punishment for telling the lie that killed Drona, your teacher, who loved you. Every king must experience hell for a little while. Now I will take you to where your loved ones are waiting for you.'

Yudhishthira entered heaven and was united with his brothers, with Draupadi and with all those that had fought and died for him. And the story of the war that had destroyed a family came to an end.

Ugrashravas said:

This is the story that I heard at Janamejaya's snake sacrifice. I heard it from the sage Vaishampayana who heard it from Vyasa who was there when it all happened. Janamejaya was the son of Parikshit who was the son of Abhimanyu who was the son of Arjuna. Janamejaya performed this sacrifice to take revenge on the snake that had killed his father.

Parikshit ruled the city of Hastinapura after his father and his uncles renounced the kingdom and set off on their final journey. Once, when he had gone hunting, he was separated from his companions. Parikshit wandered alone, hungry and thirsty until he came to the hermitage of a sage, deep in the forest. But the sage had taken a vow of silence and did not respond when the king asked him for food and water. He remained in his meditative state and that made Parikshit very angry. He picked up a dead snake that was lying in the grass and with the tip of his bow he placed it around the sage's neck and went away.

The sage's son learned that his father had been insulted in this way by the king and, in his anger, he said, 'Parikshit will die of snakebite in the next seven days. Takshaka, the king of the nagas, will be the instrument of his death!'

But the sage was not pleased when he heard what his son had done, for Parikshit was a good and just king. He immediately sent one of his disciples to Hastinapura to warn the king about the curse and to tell him to take all the precautions he could to prevent a snake from biting him.

In a single day, a new palace was constructed for the king. It stood on a sky-touching pillar that rose from a deep moat that was surrounded by priests who knew every spell to keep snakes away and to counteract their poison. Parikshit lived in the heart of the palace that was guarded at all times, all the way from his room to the outer doors. Six days passed without incident and Parikshit began to relax a little. But he did not know that Takshaka had taken the form of a young student and was making his way to Hastinapura in the company of other brahmins who were going to the city.

As the group reached the city gates, Takshaka transformed himself into a tiny worm and entered a fruit that was being taken to the king. It was sunset on the seventh day and Parikshit was laughing as he reached for a selection of fruit which was presented to him on a tray of gold. The worm emerged. Takshaka took on his own form and, as a huge serpent, he bit Parikshit on the neck. The king was dead in an instant and, in the confusion that followed, Takshaka, who had transformed himself back into a worm, disappeared.

Years later, a brahmin named Utanka, who had his own enmity with Takshaka, said to Janamejaya, 'Your father's killer wanders free and you act as if that is not important. You should conduct the great snake sacrifice that will get rid of all the wicked snakes in the three worlds. Perform this ritual without any delay and let all the snakes face the consequences of Takshaka's actions!'

Janamejaya took his advice seriously and committed himself to performing the deadly ritual. Snake after snake fell into the sacrificial fire and, eventually, Takshaka himself was drawn there by the spells recited by the priests. He hovered in the air, using all his powers to save himself from falling into the flames. When it seemed that all was lost for Takshaka, a young brahmin named Astika spoke out.

Astika said, 'I bring you a message from the gods – Brahma himself says that this is enough. Be content with the snakes that you have killed!'

Vyasa spoke to Janamejaya and said that the sacrifice had gone as far as necessary. The king obeyed the great sage and the snake sacrifice came to an end.

It was at Janamejaya's sacrifice that the story of his forefathers was recited for all to hear. And I have brought it to you, who live in this timeless forest because it is a story that will live forever.

And as Ugrashravas has been reciting what he heard from Vaishampayana who heard it from Vyasa who was there when it all happened, you, too, have been listening. You, too, have heard this marvellous story of god acting in the world of men, a story about the dawn of the last age. It is a story that must be told over and over again so that we learn that hatred will destroy us all, that arrogance and greed will lead to destruction. But it is also a story that tells us it is possible to be good and honourable. Each of us who hears this story learns that we have to make a choice about how we want to live, for what we choose determines the nature of the world. It is up to us to make sure that the seed of goodness that exists within us all does not die, not even in this last and most difficult of all ages.

Author's Note

The Mahabharata is said to be the world's longest poem, it is one hundred thousand verses long and in all its eighteen volumes it occupies the best part of a long shelf in your bookcase. Composed in Sanskrit, it is attributed to the sage Vyasa who also plays a critical role in the story that he tells. We believe that the Mahabharata started to come together about two thousand five hundred years ago, around 500 BCE, but it took many centuries and the work of many hearts and minds to become the rich and complex text that it now is. The Mahabharata contains thousands of stories, not all of them directly connected to the central narrative of the war between the Pandavas and the Kauravas. This volume is a short version of a great story, perhaps one of the greatest stories of all times.

The Mahabharata is not easy to read – its characters are driven by revenge, anger, greed, ambition and jealousy. Brother fights brother, teachers and elders are killed by those they have nurtured and loved, women are betrayed, children are sacrificed. When the war between the Pandavas and the Kauravas ends, we feel a sense of relief rather than the jubilation of victory, we mourn for the dead instead of celebrating with the living. In this story, even the god who lives as a man among humans is cursed to die alone.

The Mahabharata offers us little comfort for the present and even less hope for the future – why do we read it then, why has this story stayed with us for two and a half thousand years? It does not offer us a poignant love story as the Ramayana does, nor does it persuade us that being good is its own reward.

There are several reasons why we instinctively think of the Ramayana and the Mahabharata together. These two texts frame the Hindu understanding of moral action. They were composed around the same time, they both tell stories of men who should be king, who are sent into exile, who fight bloody battles against formidable enemies. More important, perhaps, is that we see both these men, Yudhishthira in the Mahabharata and Rama in the Ramayana, trying to understand how to be good in the world: how to be good sons, good husbands and good kings.

Both realise that it is impossible to do the right thing all the time and yet that is what they strive for. Further, they struggle with the fact that even when they do what they believe to be right, they cannot be sure that the consequences will be good for those around them. For example, being a good king often means betraying one's loved ones, as Rama does when he sends Sita to the forest because his subjects suspect her behaviour while she was Ravana's prisoner. Yudhishthira tells his first and only lie in order to shorten the war and save the lives of thousands of men – but the lie he tells causes the death of his beloved teacher.

Rama and Yudhishthira are aware that the most difficult choices are those that involve a conflict between their love for their families and their position in the world. But while Rama has to contend with his duties and obligations to people that he loves and honours, Yudhishthira has to work out how to act righteously with people for whom he has neither affection nor respect. Maybe this is why the Mahabharata keeps drawing us back to itself – we know that it is easier to do the right thing when we are motivated by the welfare of those we care about but the Mahabharata asks us to think about being good to those that hate us. Pushing our understanding of ethical dilemmas and moral judgements even further, the Mahabharata asks us to consider that good men can act dishonourably and that bad men can be motivated by justice and loyalty.

Like millions of others over the centuries, I, too, have found my way to this encyclopedia of human emotions and experience. For this retelling, I have turned to the original Sanskrit text when I needed clarity about characters and events. After a life spent with the Ramayana, I still prefer that story's belief that being good is possible but the Mahabharata has taught me a more important lesson. It has shown me how easy it is to be bad. I may not have found the answers

I seek in the Mahabharata, but I have certainly seen my questions reflected in this magnificent text. Each of us who reads this story will find something that speaks directly to them, albeit in a whisper. How could it be otherwise, for the Mahabharata says about itself, 'What is here can be found elsewhere, but what is not here is nowhere else.'

A Note on the Author

Arshia Sattar has a PhD in classical Indian literatures from the University of Chicago. She works with the Sanskrit epics and storytelling traditions of India. Her abridged translation of Valmiki's Ramayana, published in Penguin Classics, is regarded as one of the definitive presentations of the epic in English. She has written a number of books on Hindu mythology for younger readers including the bestselling *Ramayana for Children* and *Garuda and the Serpents.*

A Note on the Illustrator

Sonali Zohra has a background in fine art and photography and a master's degree in design from the University of New South Wales, Sydney. The combination of these three informs her illustration practice. Sonali works with publishers both in India and overseas. When she is not drawing, you will find her gardening, listening to music and reading in the company of her two cats.

About Juggernaut Kids

Juggernaut Kids is an exciting new imprint for Indian children which focuses on inspiring non-fiction, classic fiction and beautiful illustrations. We want to create great Indian stories for today's child.

Read Arshia Sattar's Other Books

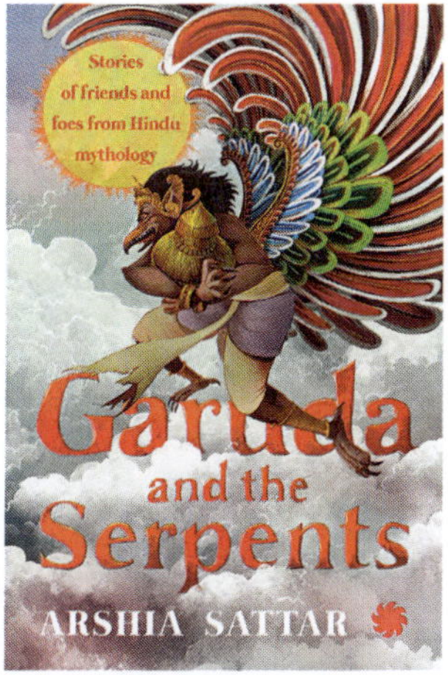

ISBN 9789386228710
224 pp
Rs 350
B/PB
For sale in the Indian Subcontinent only

ISBN 9789353450434
232 pp
Rs 499
7" × 7"/PB
For sale in the Indian Subcontinent only